INCREASING SHAREHOLDER VALUE

Distribution Policy, A Corporate Finance Challenge

INCREASING SHAREHOLDER VALUE

Distribution Policy, A Corporate Finance Challenge

by

Harold Bierman, Jr.

The Nicholas H. Noyes Professor of Business Administration
The Johnson Graduate School of Management
Cornell University
Ithaca, New York

KLUWER ACADEMIC PUBLISHERS
Boston / Dordrecht / London

Distributors for North, Central and South America:
Kluwer Academic Publishers
101 Philip Drive
Assinippi Park
Norwell, Massachusetts 02061 USA
Telephone (781) 871-6600
Fax (781) 681-9045
E-Mail <kluwer@wkap.com>

Distributors for all other countries:
Kluwer Academic Publishers Group
Distribution Centre
Post Office Box 322
3300 AH Dordrecht, THE NETHERLANDS
Telephone 31 78 6392 392
Fax 31 78 6546 474
E-Mail <services@wkap.nl>

 Electronic Services <http://www.wkap.nl>

Library of Congress Cataloging-in-Publication Data
Bierman, Harold.
   Increasing shareholder value:distribution policy, a corporate finance challenge /by
Harold Bierman, Jr.
      p.cm.
   Includes bibliographical references and index.
   ISBN 0-7923-7517-3 (alk. paper)
   1. Corporate profits. 2. Income distribution. 3. Investments--Valuation. 4.
Corporations--Finance. 5. Stockholders. I.Title

HG4028.P7 B54 2001
658.15'5--dc21

                                                                                2001038524

TABLE OF CONTENTS

Increasing Shareholder Value

Distribution Policy, a Corporate Finance Challenge

Preface

Corporations earn incomes and amass wealth. There are many books offering advice how to increase the profitability of corporations by achieving excellence in operations and choosing the correct strategic path. This book is concerned with how the corporation should reward its shareholders after the incomes are earned.

Chapters where there are potentially complex mathematical relationships are divided into two parts. The body of the chapter has the relevant basic conclusions and numerical examples. The appendices to the chapter contains the derivation of the formulas that are used, if the derivations are not relatively intuitive. The appendices can be skipped if you are willing to accept the formulas used in the chapters.

Harold Bierman, Jr.
Cornell University
Ithaca, New York

Chapter 1

An Overview of Corporate Distribution Policy

The managing director (MD) of one of the world's five largest investment banks was teaching a real live case in my finance case course. He concluded that the healthy firm being discussed should reduce or eliminate its dividend on its stock. A visiting professor who was subject to pontification raised his hand and when called on asked, in a supercilious tone, the MD whether or not he was aware that all the empirical academic research indicated that on the average the stock price of firms that reduced dividends suffered declines compared to the market and that he (the MD) mistakenly advocated a dividend decrease.

If you agree with the visiting professor that on the average dividend decreases are accompanied by negative stock price effects, you are on solid ground. However, if you conclude that therefore any specific firm should not reduce its dividend, then you should continue reading this book. Empirical studies of the effects of dividend decreases on stock prices tell us nothing about what a board of directors should decide on reviewing a specific firm's dividend policy.

The Choices

Business corporations attempt to make profits and increase the value of the stockholder's position. Management makes capital structure, working capital, investment, marketing, operations and personnel decisions with that objective in mind. But there is one important element missing in the above listing. How should the equity investors be rewarded?

This book focuses on the distribution policy decisions of corporations as they affect shareholders. After a corporation makes a profit what is the best way to transmit the benefits to the shareholders? What is the economic importance to investors of this distribution decision?

In choosing a distribution policy a corporation has a wide range of choices. This book will consider the following alternatives:

1.   Retained earnings
2.   Cash dividends
3.   Share repurchase
4.   Dividend reinvestment plan (DRIP)
5.   Stock dividends
6.   Sale of business (combined with retained earnings)
7.   Bond interest
8.   Preferred stock dividends

It probably is not obvious why all of the above items are included. The above list has to be explained. We will, at times, shift the firm's objective from maximizing the value of the stockholder's position to increasing the firm's value to all its capital investors.

This latter objective will be consistent with maximizing the value of the stockholders, but will be somewhat broader.

Chapter 2

Dividends Versus Retained Earnings

This chapter assumes a corporation has excess cash and retained earnings. We will only consider two alternatives:

a.　　the corporation pays a cash dividend

b.　　the corporation adds to its retained earnings.

The term "excess cash" means the corporation has cash in excess of maintenance capital expenditures and high priority other capital expenditures. Should it pay a cash dividend? Black (1976) defined the puzzle that exists since corporations pay dividends when logic seems to indicate that they should not.

A corporation is not legally obligated to declare a dividend of any specific amount. Thus, a firm's board of directors actually has made a specific distribution decision every time a dividend is declared. However, once the board declares a dividend, the corporation is legally obligated to make the payments. Therefore, a dividend should not be declared unless a corporation is in a financial position to make the payment.

The expectation of receiving dividends (broadly defined as any distribution of value) ultimately determines the market value of the common stock. By declaring a dividend, the board of directors is not only turning over some of the assets of the corporation to its stockholders, but it may be influencing the expectations that stockholders have about the future dividends they can expect from the corporation. If expectations are affected, the dividend decision and the underlying dividend policy will have an impact on the value that the market places on the common stock of the corporation.

Many financial experts believe that a stable dividend results in a higher stock price. A common reason for this belief is that some stockholders prefer a steady cash flow stream from their investments. There is at least one other reason for thinking that a variable dividend rate may not be in the best interest of a company. In the long run, the value of a share of stock tends to be determined by the discounted value of the expected dividends or other cash flows. Insofar as this is the case, a fluctuating dividend rate will tend to make it difficult for the prospective stockholders to determine the value of the stock and the stock is likely to sell at a lower price than comparable stocks paying the same average dividend through time but making the payments at a steady rate. This conclusion assumes that investors are risk averse and have incomplete information about the company.

Factors Affecting Investor Reaction to Dividends

Traditional concepts about the distinction between income and capital, some of which have been embodied into laws that control the behavior of certain financial institutions, are important considerations in understanding how these investors react to corporate dividend decisions and policies. The more recent and sophisticated thinking about financial matters tends to emphasize the total return received from an asset and to ignore distinction between capital gains and other forms of income except insofar as they affect taxes. Thus, we will focus on the tax consequences of alternative strategies.

Suppose that an investor held shares of Company A and shares of Company B. At the beginning of the year, the shares in both of the companies were selling for $50. During the year, Company A paid a dividend of $3 per share, and the stock was selling for $52 a share at the end of the year. Company B paid no dividend but the stock in that company was selling for $56 per share at the end of the year. The total return approach considers that the stockholders had received a return of $5 per share from Company A and $6 a share from Company B. The next step is to consider the after-tax returns from the two investments.

The total return approach treats the market value of the securities held and dividends received as one pool of liquid assets that can be divided up at each decision point into consumption and further investment. The fact that some of the liquid assets available have come from dividends and others from a change in the value of the investment would be of secondary importance if there were no taxes and no transaction costs.

There are some investors who approach these same events with a very different point of view and conclude that there is an important distinction between income and capital gains. Stockholder return is typically defined as the sum of dividends and interest. Investors who think of only dividends as the return often are quite comfortable in consuming part or all of their dividend but are very uncomfortable about having to dispose of some of their securities in order to consume.

If dividends are considered to be the only income from common stock, and if this concept is embodied in legal concepts, then the amount of cash dividends will tend to influence the likelihood of a company's shares being purchased by this segment of the market.

Suppose that a wealthy man specifies in his will that the income from his estate is to go to his wife during her lifetime but that the capital is to be preserved and applied for the benefit of their children after his wife passes away. If the estate is large, a bank trust department will frequently be appointed as trustee to carry out the intentions of the person creating the will. There are billions of dollars of assets managed by bank trust departments under the terms of trust agreements that are basically similar to the one described. In many of these cases, only dividends and interest are considered to be income.

The distinction between dividends and capital gains is also reinforced by tax laws that define the receipt of dividends or interest as a taxable event. By contrast, changes in the value of common stock are not taxable events unless, and until, the securities are actually sold.

One further institutional factor that should be mentioned in connection with dividends is the so-called trust legal list. Banks, insurance companies, and other financial institutions, as well as individual trustees, often manage substantial sums for the benefit of others. Over the years, many states have passed laws designed to ensure that the beneficiaries of these assets do not incur losses because trustees have purchased excessively risky investments for the trust. Various controls have been designed to accomplish this end. One is to restrict the kinds of assets that are eligible for considerations investments by a particular kind of trustee or financial institution. Such a list of eligible assets is called a trust legal list. The laws do not specify the particular securities that are eligible for inclusion on the legal list but rather the characteristics that a security must possess in order to be eligible. A state official is responsible for determining which securities have the necessary characteristics. To be eligible for inclusion on a legal list, a common stock may need to have paid dividends without interruption for a given length of time. A consequence of this procedure is that if a company fails to pay dividends, this policy may substantially reduce the population of investors who are eligible to buy or hold its common stock.

Corporate Dividend Practice

There have been a number of important studies dealing with the actual behavior of corporations in setting dividend policy. A classic study was conducted by the late Harvard economist John Lintner (1956). Lintner found that two considerations account for a large part of the actual behavior of corporations. One consideration was the desire to have a relatively stable dividend; the second was the desire to pay out, in the long run, a constant fraction of earnings. This fraction is usually referred to as the payout target. These objectives may be conflicting. Earnings tend to fluctuate substantially from year to year. If a corporation routinely paid out a given fraction of those earnings as dividends, then the dividend itself would tend to fluctuate drastically from year to year or quarter to quarter. These fluctuations would conflict with the objective of maintaining a stable dividend amount. On the other hand, if the dividend is a constant amount, then it will be a fluctuating proportion of earnings.

Companies vary the payout ratio they select, and the speed with which they adjust the dividend of a period to changes in earnings, but they do tend to adhere to a target payout ratio. Over long periods of time, this policy tends to result in a dividend payout that is approximately equal to the payout target, but dividends will tend to be more stable from year to year than earnings. Another important consequence of this process is that dividend decisions tend to provide information to stockholders about management's forecasts of future earnings. This signal might not be reliable.

Assume that a firm has a large amount of desirable investments and that these investments require more funds than are available internally after dividend commitments have been met. In such circumstances, there are three major alternatives. First, is a reduction in the dividend amount. Secondly, the company might forgo some profitable investments. The third alternative is to seek additional funds. The choice of the best path is likely to be based on subjective evaluations of the consequences.

If the dividend payout ratio is set too low, relative to the level of earnings and the quantity of profitable investments available to it, the company may either find itself accumulating an unwarranted amount of liquid assets or be tempted to accept investments that are not consistent with the objective of maximizing the economic well-being of the stockholders. The stock of a company that invests in undesirable investments is likely to be depressed compared to its potential value. Another possibility is for the company to invest in other corporations that it considers fairly valued.

The Setting of Dividend Policy

A well-defined dividend policy provides the investors a clear basis of choice. Investors knowing the dividend policies of the alternative companies can choose the type of company that best fits their individual investment goals. This is desirable, because stockholders differ in the extent to which they prefer dividends rather than opportunities for capital appreciation. One must remember that while one group might well prefer capital gains, a second group of zero-tax investors may be interested in dividends as well as capital gains. This second group of investors includes universities, foundations, and private pension funds, all of which accrue no special tax advantages from capital gains as distinct from dividends.

Sometimes a company will distinguish between a "regular" dividend and an "extra" dividend. Although this distinction does not have any cash flow significance, it is a means by which the directors can signal their intentions to stockholders. By labeling part of a dividend payment as an "extra", the directors are indicating that they did not necessarily expect to continue those payments in future years. By declaring the remainder of the dividend payment as a regular payment, the directors indicate an intention to maintain this dividend for the foreseeable future. When used, extra dividends tend to occur in the fourth quarter of a good earnings year. In recent years share repurchasing has virtually eliminated the practice of paying extra dividends.

Dividend Changes and Earnings Forecasts

The fact that an increase has not been declared may sometimes be interpreted as evidence that management does not expect the current level of earnings to be increased. On the other had, if a dividend increase takes place at a time when it is not expected, the financial community may interpret this as evidence that management is more bullish about future prospects for the company than had previously been expected.

The stock price effect that can occur when a dividend change is unexpected is dramatically indicated by the history of the Consolidated Edison Corporation. Consolidated Edison's regular dividend in 1973 was $.45 per share per quarter. In the spring of 1974, the board of directors decided not to declare a dividend. This took place in a context in which the earnings of public utilities were being adversely affected in a dramatic way by a combination of large increases in the cost of fuel, reduction in consumption of electricity, and increases in the cost of new additions to plant and equipment. Since Consolidated Edison was one of the largest utilities in the United States and was previously considered a very safe common stock investment, its announcement of no dividend payment had a dramatic impact on the share prices of almost all privately owned electric utility companies in the United States. Consolidated Edison shares dropped from a preannouncement level of around $21.00 to a post-announcement low of about $6.00 per share. The market took the elimination of the dividend by Con Ed to be a forecast by management that the firm and the industry faced severe financial difficulties and introduced a level of risk into the investors' analysis that in their view previously did not exist.

Dividend Policy, Investment Policy, and Financing Policy

The dividend policy of a firm cannot be considered in isolation from its other financial policies. In particular, dividend policy is intimately connected with investment policy and financing policy. When a firm changes its dividend amount, it may, at the same time, have to change one or the other of these other policies. If the firm increased its dividend, it would be necessary for it, at the same time, to generate more cash flow from operations, to sell assets, to issue debt or senior equity, or to reduce its expenditures on new plant, equipment, and working capital or some combination of the above.

A firm has a set of investment opportunities that are expected to be available. It also has a cost of equity capital. The investment alternatives may be ranked (not easily) where additional investment opportunities will be less profitable than the best alternatives.

The firm wishes to invest up to the point at which the marginal rate of return on the stockholder's equity investment equals the cost of equity. It would not want to invest stockholder capital in projects earning less than its cost of equity.

If the firm anticipates that its cash flows from operations will exceed the amount needed to undertake all desirable investments, then it has cash with which it can pay a dividend from the cash flow from operations. But should a dividend be paid?

In any particular year it would be surprising if the amount of cash generated internally and the schedule of available investment opportunities were exactly as anticipated. Thus, some temporary adjustments are needed. The firm can adjust its dividend policy, its capital structure policy, or its investment policy, including investing in other corporations. It will try to make the adjustments that are least costly to it long-term objectives.

A firm may not reduce a well-established dividend as a means of coping with a temporary shortage of cash. It might prefer to adjust its capital budget or raise debt or preferred stock capital.

Irrelevance of Dividend Policy

Miller and Modigliani (1961) showed that dividend policy is not relevant in determining the value of a firm if some well-defined conditions are met. The conditions include:

1. Perfect capital markets (including rational investors, perfect information avail-able to all and certainty).
2. No transaction costs.
3. Investors are not taxed.
4. The investment policy of the firm is set and the amount invested is not affected by the dividend policy.

Assume a firm intends to invest $100 and it has generated $100 of income. It could retain the $100 and the investors have an increased $100 investment in the firm. But assume the firm pays a $100 dividend. To invest $100 it must obtain $100 from its stockholders. After the stockholders invest $100 in the firm the net change in the stockholders cash is zero, and the stockholders with the dividend are in the identical financial situation as the stockholders when zero dividends were paid. Our conclusion will change when investor taxes are introduced.

However, if some of the assumptions stated are relaxed, the conclusion that the amount of dividends paid (or more exactly, the dividend policy) is irrelevant in determining the present value of the common stock is not true. For example:

1. If transaction costs paid by the firm in raising new capital are substantial, the firm with investment opportunities that exceed its positive cash flow will incur larger transaction costs if dividends are paid, since more capital must be raised; also; investor not in need of funds would prefer to avoid paying transaction costs to reinvest the dividend proceeds.
2. Since capital gains are not taxed until realized by stockholders, and the tax rate on long term capital gains is less than the tax rate on ordinary (dividend) income, tax-paying stockholders who do not need funds or who can obtain the funds they need by selling securities may prefer smaller dividends and more retained earnings; in

this respect, earnings retention can be viewed as a method of tax deferment and tax reduction.

Income Taxes and Dividend Policy

The income taxes of stockholders should affect the dividend policy of a firm. We shall first examine the importance of tax deferral and then show the impact of having two different tax rates, one for ordinary income and one for capital gains.

Rational stockholders should value a stock based on the after-tax returns they expect to receive from owning it. The tax status of the return from invested capital depends on the form in which it is received. The provisions of the U.S. tax code tend to lead to a situation that, among a group of securities with similar risks, high-tax individuals should prefer stocks whose returns are in the form of capital gains. Also, by comparative advantage, pension funds should find that they can do better by holding stocks whose returns are in the form of dividends. There is some evidence that this occurs in practice. Pension funds managed by bank trust departments have stocks with a higher average dividend payout ratio than do personal trust funds (whose beneficiaries tend to have relatively high marginal tax rates) managed by the same banks (see U.S. Securities and Exchange Commission, 1971).

The returns received by pension funds and by other nontaxable entities are not subject to either ordinary income or capital gains taxes at the time. Thus, managers of pension funds value stocks based on the before-tax returns they expect to receive from them.

Tax Deferral Advantage

We want to consider the effect on the stockholders' wealth at the end of one period if a company, instead of paying a dividend, retains the same amount and reinvests it to earn a return of r after corporate taxes and then pays a cash dividend at time 1. This policy will be compared to a policy of paying a dividend to the stockholders, having it taxed and then having the stockholders invest the after-tax dividend after-tax return in the capital market.

A typical corporation is faced with the fact that it has stockholders with widely different tax rates. Both pension funds (with zero tax rates) and high-tax investors will own the common stock of the same corporation. Nevertheless, we can determine the gain or loss to an investor of different dividend policies using the calculation methods of this chapter.

A cash dividend has two drawbacks. One, it is taxed immediately and secondly it is taxed at the ordinary income tax rate. Effectively, the immediate taxation leads to a reinvestment at the after-tax return available in the capital market while the retained earnings earn the corporate after-tax return which is before investor tax.

A One Period Example

Let us compute the deferral advantage of a corporation reinvesting $100 for one year to earn .10 compared to paying a dividend of $100. The stockholders can earn .06 after tax on external investments and they do not need current funds. Assume that the personal marginal tax rate on ordinary income is .396. With an immediate $100 dividend after one year the investor earning .06 after tax has:

$$(1-.396)\,(100)\,(1.06) = \$64.024$$

With retention by the corporation earning .10 and then a dividend the investor nets

$$(1-.396)\,(100)\,(1.10) = \$66.44$$

The retention alternative yields $66.44 to the stockholders at the end of the year compared to $64.024 if the dividend is paid.

If capital gains are taxed at .20 and if the retention of $100 leads to a capital gain of $110 at the end of the year the investor has

$$(1-.2)\,100(1.10) = \$88.$$

The retention alternative with the capital gains tax rate yields $88 to the stockholders at the end of the year compared to $64.024 if the dividend is paid.

A 40 Year Example

The economic advantage of retention compared to a dividend is more dramatic if the time horizon is lengthened. Assume a 40 year time horizon and again the corporation has $100 which it can invest to earn .10 or give the $100 to investors who can earn .06. With a $100 dividend the investor will have $621.26:

$$(1-.396)\ 100(1.06)^{40} = \$621.26$$

with retention and then a capital gain the investor will have:

$$(1-.20)\ 100(1.10)^{40} = \$3,620.74.$$

The relative size of the return that can be earned by the investor (.06) and that can be earned by the corporation (.10) affects the relative advantages of retention. The difference in the investor's wealth caused by the choice of dividend or retention can be large (as illustrated above).

The Firm Value

Assume a firm will earn $1,000,000 a year of basic earnings (after corporate income tax). If the firm pays a $1,000,000 dividend per year, after 40 years the investor will have:

$$(1-.396)\ 1,000,000\ F(40, .06) = \$93,476,000$$

where F(40, .06) is the future value of an annuity of $1 per year and

$$F(40, .06) = \frac{(1.06)^{40} - 1}{.06} = \$154.76$$

Now assume the $1,000,000 per year is retained to earn .10 and at the end of 40 years the value of the retentions is sold and the investors have a capital gain:

$$(1-.20)\ 1,000,000\ F(40, .10) = \$354,074,000$$

With retention the value to investors is increased by 3.76 times compared to an immediate dividends each year. If the corporation had very special investment opportunities so that it earned more than .10 per year the advantages of retentions would be even more dramatic. Also, the .20 capital gains tax can be avoided by the investor not realizing the capital gain at time 40.

Cost of Retained Earnings

Because investors are taxed, the cost of retained earnings is less than the cost of new equity capital. The cost of retained earnings is the return that retained earnings would have to earn on reinvestment in order for stockholders to be indifferent between the immediate receipt of the funds as a dividend and their retention. Here we assume zero transaction costs and that all investor income is taxed at the ordinary tax rate of t_p.

To calculate the cost of retained earnings, we examine the change in stockholders' wealth under the assumption that if reinvestment of $1 takes place at an after-corporate-tax rate of r, the investment leads to a value of $(1 + r)$. Assume the entire proceeds to the investor are taxed as ordinary income of a rate of t_p. The after-tax change in stockholders' wealth after one time period will be

$$(1+r)\ (1-t_p)$$

per dollar of reinvested funds.

If the $1 dividend payment were to take place immediately and, after payment of ordinary income taxes on it at rate t_p, the residual funds were reinvested in the capital markets in securities of equivalent risk earning r_p after personal tax, the net change in stockholders' wealth per dollar of dividend paid is:

$$(1-t_p)(1+r_p)$$

where r_p is the after-investor-tax return on the invested funds.

Define the cost of retained earnings, r, to be the rate of return that the firm must earn on reinvested funds for stockholder indifference between a dividend and retention. Equating the after-tax change in stockholder wealth per dollar of funds under the two alternatives we find that $r = r_p$. It can be shown that this result is independent of the number of time periods. If the firm can earn the same return as stockholders can earn after tax, stockholders would be indifferent between having the firm pay a dividend and reinvest the funds, and this is the definition of the cost of retained earnings. If investors can earn .06 after tax in the capital markets then the firm must earn at least .06 to justify retention.

If new capital is being obtained, the investor has a choice between having \$1 in hand or investing in a firm that will earn r and pay r dividend with an after-tax value of $(1-t_p)r$. Using r_p as the discount rate the after tax benefit has a present value of $r(1-t_p)/r_p$. Equating the two alternatives of having \$1 or investing in the corporation and solving for r, we now have:

$$1 = \frac{r\left(1-t_p\right)}{r_p}$$

$$r = \frac{r_p}{1-t_p} \qquad (1)$$

where r_p is the after tax return available to investors, t_p is the tax rate on ordinary income and r is the minimum after corporate tax return the corporation must earn to justify retention.

With retained earnings, the cost of stockholders' equity capital was the after tax return (r_p) available in the market. With new capital being obtained, the cost of stockholders' equity is now increased. If r_p = .06 and t_p = .396:

$$r = \frac{r_p}{1-t_p} = \frac{.06}{1-.396} = .0993.$$

Having established the fact that the cost of stockholders' equity depends on whether the firm is retaining earnings or whether the firm is obtaining new capital we could next introduce capital gains taxes and the decision by the investor to hold or sell. These factors will also affect the cost of equity capital. Thus, the cost of equity capital, rather than being one easily determined number, is a function of the tax law and the decisions of investors. The solution offered by equation (1) is an approximate solution since corporations will typically pay dividends and retain earnings simultaneously. However, equation (1) does illustrate the fact that the cost of stockholders' equity funds depend on the source of the capital being invested as well as on the dividend policy of the firm.

Dividends: The Clientele Effect

Theory says that zero-tax investors will prefer high-dividend-yield stocks and the high-tax investors will prefer zero- or low-dividend-yield stocks. This implies that dividend policy will affect the types of investors (the clientele) who will own a company's stock. Researchers have attempted to estimate the effects of dividends on stock prices.

Litzenberger and Ramaswamy (1979 and 1982) found that higher-dividend-yielding stocks tend to have higher expected returns. However, Black and Scholes (1979) and Miller and Scholes (1982) do not find that dividends have any effect on the stocks' expected return. Thus, the empirical evidence is not definitive. One thing is certain: no one has proved that dividend policy does not affect stock prices. It is useful to think about the prospective economic consequences of different policies.

Reasons for Dividends

There are many reasons for a firm to pay dividends. Some of these have been illustrated in the models of the preceding sections. These reasons include:

1. The firm generates more cash internally than can be profitable reinvested.
2. Dividends provide stable "income" to investors (they can plan assuming the dividends will be paid). If dividends were not paid and investors needed money, they would have to sell stock.
3. The Internal Revenue Service penalizes unnecessary retained earnings (this provision is frequently not applied).
4. Transaction costs associated with an investor selling stock make dividends less costly if the investor needs cash income.
5. Other firms pay dividends.
6. Trust legal lists (eligible securities for trusts) require a record of continuous dividend payments).
7. Some investors pay zero or very low taxes, and there is little or no tax advantage in deferred income taxes to this group.
8. If a firm has been paying a dividend, it is difficult to stop paying a dividend without hurting some stock-holders. Investors expect dividends and cessation of dividends would be a negative signal to investors.
9. Nonpayment of dividends may encourage "raiders".
10. A market that heavily discounts the risky future (reflecting a high degree of uncertainty) will value current dividend payments more than future dividend payments. Dividends reduce risk.
11. A large dividend growth rate attracts analysts

The primary reasons for dividends are zero or low tax rates for the investors and the investors want cash. The trust legal list aspect is important only if the firm wants its stock included in trust portfolios. The other reasons listed are very weak.

The primary arguments against dividends are that the retained earnings save flotation costs compared to a new issue, and in addition, the payment of a dividend causes the stockholder to be taxed immediately at ordinary rates on the amount of cash received while retained earnings offer the prospect of capital gains in the future and lower tax rates. Since some investors prefer to defer taxes, one way to do so is to have the firm retain and reinvest earnings. Furthermore, there is a distinct tax advantage in having capital gains rather than ordinary income since capital gains are taxed at a lower rate than ordinary income and some of the cash proceeds are protected from taxes.

Floatation costs are of two types. First are the out-of-pocket expenses: legal fees, underwriters' commission, and so on. Second is the discount that must be offered to ensure that the issue is sold. Existing shareholders may suffer from dilution (the second type of expense) unless the stock is sold to them.

Conclusions

We first examined the relevancy of a dividend policy with zero taxes and zero transaction costs. Under these very special conditions, which are not likely to hold in the real world, the market value of a firm's stock was shown to be independent of its dividend policy. Next, we examined the institutional factors and investor characteristics that determine the effect of dividend policy on the market value of the stock. It seems that different firms might wish to adopt different dividend policies, depending on the economic and the behavioral characteristics of their stockholders and the investors they wish to attract.

If investors in a high tax bracket expect the price of a stock to increase because of improved earnings (and a higher level of future cash flows), they will be willing to pay more for a stock knowing that if their expectations are realized the stock can be sold and be taxed at the relatively lower capital gains tax rate, than if immediate cash dividends are to be paid. Whereas the capital gains tax treatment tends to increase the value of a share of stock, we have shown that another powerful factor arises from the ability of the stockholder to defer paying taxes if the corporation retains income rather than paying dividends. Tax deferral is an extremely important advantage associated with the retention of earnings by a corporation.

The present tax law allows deferral of tax payment (or complete avoidance) on capital gains, and recognized gains are taxed at a lower (.20) rate than ordinary income (.396 at the maximum). Dividend policies of firms have relevance for public policy in the areas of taxation of both corporation and individuals. As corporate managers adjust their decision making to include the tax law considerations, the makers of public policy must decide whether the results are beneficial to society.

It is not being argued that all firms should discontinue dividends payments. There is a place for a variety of payout policies, but there is a high cost to investors for all firms attempting to cater to the dividend and reinvestment preferences of an average investor. The firm that combines dividend payments with the issuance of securities to current investors is causing some of its investors to pay unnecessary taxes, as well as incurring increased transactions costs itself in raising the funds.

A board of directors acting in the interests of the stockholders of a corporation sets the dividend policy of a firm. The ability of an investor to defer income taxes as a result of the company retaining earnings is an important consideration. In addition, the distinction between ordinary income and capital gains for purpose of income taxation by the federal government accentuates the importance of investors knowing the dividend policy of the firm whose stock they are considering purchasing or have already purchased. In turn, this means that the corporation (and its board) has a responsibility to announce its dividend policy, and attempt to be consistent in its policy, changing only when its economic situation changes significantly. In the particular situation in which a firm is expanding its investments rapidly and is financing this expansion by issuing securities to its stockholders, the payment of cash dividends is especially vulnerable to criticism.

The planning of investment decisions, capital structure, and dividend policy must be coordinated so that the well being of the firm's stockholders is incorporated in the planning process. The corporate planners should realize that the individual investors are also making plans, and the corporation can assist this planning process by making its own financial plans and strategies well known.

References

Black, F. and M. Scholes, "The Effects of Dividend Yield and Dividend Policy in Common Stock Prices and Returns," *Journal of Financial Economics*, 1 (May 1979), pp. 1-22.

Black, F., "The Dividend Puzzle," *Journal of Portfolio Management*, (1976), pp. 5-8.

Lintner, J., "Distribution of Income of Corporations Among Dividends, Retained Earnings and Taxes," *American Economic Review*, Mary 1956, pp. 97-113.

Litzenberger, R.H. and K. Ramaswamy, "The Effect of Personal Taxes and Dividends on Capital Asset Prices: Theory and Empirical Evidence," *Journal of Financial Economics*, 7 (June, 1979), pp. 163-195.

Litzenberger, R.H. and K. Ramaswamy, "The Effects of Dividends on Common Stock Prices: Tax Effects or Information Effects," *Journal of Finance*, 37 (May 1982), pp. 429-443.

Miller, M. and F. Modigliani, "Dividend Policy, Growth and the Value of Shares," *Journal of Business*, 34 (October 1961), pp. 411-433.

Miller, M. and M. Scholes, "Dividends and Taxes: No Empirical Evidence", *Journal of Political Economy*, 90(1982) pp 118-1141.

U.S. Securities and Exchange Commission, *Institutional Investor Study Report*, Chapter IX, "Distribution and Characteristics of Holdings in Institutional Portfolios" (Washington D.C., Government Printing Office, 1971), pp. 1330-1331.

Chapter 3

Dividends Versus Share Repurchase

In the past four decades, major U.S. corporations have increasingly repurchased significant amounts of their own common shares. The reasons for this development and its implications for the theory of share valuation and for public policy, however, have been subject to numerous, and often conflicting interpretations.

The repurchase of shares is not legal under all codes of law, but in the countries where it is legal, it opens up a variety of opportunities for gains to stockholders. The motivations for repurchase are diverse. For example, assume a desire to shrink the size of the firm, with desirable consequences both for the stockholders who receive the cash distribution and for those who do not. But it is also possible for one group of investors to use share repurchase to take advantage of information that is not available to or that is misunderstood by the remainder of the investing public. The repurchase of shares is common and, barring changes in legislation, is likely to continue to have a larger growth rate in the future than cash dividends.

During the past 40 years corporations have acquired significant amounts of their own shares of common stock. The repurchase of common stock has been said to have been motivated by many factors. Among these are:

1. Repurchased stock can be used by the corporation for such reasons as mergers and acquisitions of firms, stock options and stock purchase plans, and so on.
2. Stock repurchase is a form of investment by the corporation.
3. Repurchasing stock increases the amount of financial leverage employed by the firm.
4. Stock repurchase is a method of shrinking the size of the firm (a form of liquidating dividend).

5.   Repurchase of stock compared to a cash dividend may improve financial measures such as earnings per share and, consequently, the price of the stock.

6.   Different expectations held by the firm and the market can lead, through repurchase, to improving the wealth position of current stockholders.

7.   Stock repurchase is a flexible dividend. The shareholders who do not want cash do not sell.

8.   Stock repurchase is a form of dividend, and, this form of dividend payment has favorable tax consequences compared with ordinary dividends.

We shall consider each of these reasons separately, even though several of them are interrelated. The above is not a complete listing of reasons why corporations repurchase their shares.

Repurchase of Stock for Use by the Corporation

Corporation use shares of their own stock for several purposes, including the issuance of stock options to management and the acquisition of other corporations. However, this is not a complete explanation as to why a corporation repurchases its own shares, since a corporation is generally able to issue new shares for the types of purposes for which the shares are said to be acquired.

There may be a valid reason why a corporation does not want to issue new additional shares, and so it repurchases shares for subsequent reissue. But this is not likely to be the primary reason for the large expansion in the usage of share repurchase by corporations. There is no question that it is a motivation.

Stock Repurchase as an Investment

Strictly speaking a corporation cannot "invest" in its own shares. With the normal investment, cash is converted into working assets. Profitable investments increase the size of the firm, and they may be accompanied by increases in the debt or equity accounts; they are never accompanied by decreases in these accounts at the time of the investment. However, if a firm repurchases its own shares, there is disinvestment by the corporation. With the firm's purchase of its own shares, the assets decrease as cash is used, and the stockholders' equity also decreases. The corporate entity does not make an investment when shares are acquired.

It is possible for one group of stockholders to benefit and one group to be harmed by the purchase of shares. The group not selling may increase the relative size of its investment in the firm compared to the investment of the selling group, but this is not the same as saying that the firm is actually committing resources to productive activities. Rather, share repurchase is a situation where the firm is becoming smaller as the result of the repurchase, but the relative proportion of ownership of the non-selling shareholders will increase.

The fact that the process of stock repurchase is not "investing" does not mean that the utilization of funds to purchase (retire) outstanding stock may not be the best use of the funds from the viewpoint of some or all of the stockholders. In many cases share repurchase is the best use of corporate cash (especially if the investment in other corporations is precluded.)

Increases in Financial Leverage

It is true that repurchase of shares leads to a reduction in the shareholders' investment in the firm and will lead to an increase in the ratio of debt to total stockholders' equity employed and thus will increase the amount of financial leverage. However, this increase in leverage cannot be the sole explanation of the stock repurchase process, since a cash dividend of the same amount would have an identical leverage effect. Leverage can also be increased by issuing debt. The primary explanation of stock repurchase must be found elsewhere.

Shrinking the Size of the Firm

If the objective is to shrink the size of the firm, the tax-effect rationale for using stock repurchase compared to cash dividends would lead stockholders to prefer share repurchase. Although shrinkage of the stock equity can be accomplished by a cash dividend, stock repurchase leads to part of the return being treated as a tax-free return of capital and the residual gain is taxed at the capital gains tax rate rather than ordinary income tax rate. Normally corporations do not attempt to become smaller, but rather shrinkage in size occurs because of other objectives or unfavorable events.

Improving Financial Measures

The effect of stock repurchase on financial measures and the stock price are obviously of interest to the stockholders. We shall attempt to determine the conditions under which changes in the measures take place and how the stock price is affected.

1. *Book value*: If the market price paid for the common stock is less than the current book value, the book value per share will increase for the remaining shares. However, if the market price is more than the book value, the book value will decrease if shares are repurchased. It would be surprising if such book value changes are sufficient justification for acquiring shares.

2. *Earnings per share and market price of stock*: Earnings per share will increase if the firm repurchases shares rather than pays an equal sized cash dividend. Consider a firm that currently has D dollars available for distribution either in the form of a cash dividend or stock repurchase. The investors are not taxed. If N is the number of shares outstanding prior to the repurchase and the firm pays P dollars per share to purchase D/P shares, the number of shares after repurchase will be (N-D/P) rather than N shares if a cash dividend is paid. Since D is going to be distributed in either case, the firm's future earning stream is unaffected and consequent earnings per share will be higher if the repurchase strategy is followed rather than a cash dividend. Although the earnings per share will be higher under repurchase, fewer shares will be outstanding, and with these simplified conditions one would expect the total value of the common stock to be the same under either distribution strategy. If the value of the firm and the total earnings are both unaffected, then the firm's price/earnings multiple is unaffected. Applying the same price/earnings multiple to the

higher earnings per share, however, leads to a higher market price per share.

Example
        Assume that a company currently earning (and expecting to continue to earn) $1,000,000 per year net income now has 1,000,000 shares outstanding. Further, assume that the price/earnings multiplier is 10 and that the firm has excess cash of $2,000,000 that can be used to pay a cash dividend or reacquire stock. The earnings component of the stock is worth $10 per share ($1 per share with a multiple of 10), and the excess cash adds $2 to that value. The stock has as $12 value. If a $2 per share dividend is paid and if the investors are not taxed the stock will be worth $10 ex-dividend. If the stock is repurchased before the dividend it must be repurchased at $12 per share and the firm can purchase $2,000,000 ÷ 12 or 166,667 shares.

Table 1: **Comparing a Cash Dividend and Stock Repurchase**

	Cash Dividend	Repurchase of Stock
Earnings	$1,000,000	$1,000,000
Number of shares (after repurchase)	1,000,000	833,333
EPS (after cash distribution)	$1.00	$1.20
Price/earnings multiplier	10	10
Price per share	$10.00	$12.00
Market value of stock[a]	$10,000,000	$10,000,000

[a]Number of shares times price per share.

        The Table shows the earnings per share, price per share, and total market value of the firm under the two alternatives.
        Consider an investor who owns one share of stock. If a $2 cash dividend is paid, the wealth position is $2 in dividends plus $10 in stock or $12 total. If stock is repurchased, the investor who sells before or after the repurchase receives $12; the investor who does not sell has a share of stock worth $12 after the repurchase. Thus, with no personal tax considerations, either distribution alternative is equally acceptable to an investor.   Existing tax legislation affecting investors favors repurchase.

Although the Internal Revenue Service will not allow the distribution to be treated as a capital gain if the firm repurchases stock pro rata (so that ownership proportions do not change), it will allow other forms of repurchase (e.g., open market purchases or tendering) to be treated as capital gains. There is also another factor that may influence the method of distributing cash. Suppose that you are a manager of the firm and that you have a stock option to buy stock at $11 and the current market price is $12 (this is the expected price before the cash distribution). If the $2 cash dividend is paid, it can be expected that the price of the stock will fall to about $10 (the EPS are $1 and the price/earnings multiple is 10). If the stock is repurchased, the number of shares will decrease, the EPS will be $1.20, and the price will be $12. A series of stock repurchases will tend to drive the price of the common stock upward compared to the price with a cash dividend and make it easier for the stock option to be exercised under favorable circumstances. Thus stock repurchase is a logical strategy for firms whose policies are administered by managers holding stock options. Retaining earnings rather than paying cash dividends is another desirable strategy tending to increase the price of a share of stock higher than it would be if the cash were distributed in the form of a cash dividend. Whether or not the total value is enhanced by share repurchase rather than a dividend is discussed later in this chapter.

Different Expectations

A situation may arise in which the market assesses the value of the stock differently from management's assessment, not because of different information but rather because of different expectations. If management thinks that the stock is under priced, repurchase of the stock will benefit those who continue to hold the stock if management's assessment is proved correct.

Example
Suppose that the following facts apply:

Earnings	$1,000,000
Earnings per share	$1

Number of shares	1,000,000
Market value	$8,000.000
Cash available for distribution	$2,000,000
Current market price of stock	$8
Management's projected price/earnings ratio	$10
Management's intrinsic value	$12 ($10 of capitalized earnings plus $2 excess cash)

The current P/E ratio is 8, but the capitalized earnings component of the $8 stock price is six times $1 per share or $6; the remaining $2 of value per share is the prorated value of the $2 per share cash available to be distributed. If the firm is able to repurchase the stock at $8 per share, 250,000 shares will be repurchased with the firm's $2,000,000 excess cash. Assuming that everyone had the same information, but only the conclusions (the expectations and the analyses) differ, then the persons selling are not harmed since the stock is still at a price at least as high as it would have been if the company had not been buying. The nonselling stockholders will benefit if the management is correct since there will be fewer shares outstanding. After the repurchase of 250,000 shares the remaining stockholders would have earnings per share of

$$\text{EPS} = \frac{\$1,000,000}{750,000} = \$1.33$$

If management is correct and a price/earning ratio of 10 applies to the basic earning stream, the projected market value of a share after the repurchase will be

Projected market value = 10 x $1.33 = $13.30 per share

However, if the price/earnings ratio of 6 applies, the market value will be $8.00 per share, and those who sell at $8 and those who hold will be in equivalent financial positions (ignoring taxes and transactions costs). There is no reason to think that management's projected P/E of 10 will actually occur.

Assume management thinks $12 per share is the stock's intrinsic value and management pays this price for 166,667 shares and there will be 833,333 shares outstanding. The revised earnings per share will be:

$$EPS = \frac{\$1,000,000}{833,333} = \$1.20$$

If the price/earnings ratio increases from its current value of 6 to 10, the market price per share would be $12 per share, and those selling their stock and those holding are in equivalent financial position. However, if the price/earnings ratio remains at a value of 6, the price per share would be $7.20 per share and the persons selling their common stock for $12 per share would be better off financially than those holding the stock.

Thus, if management is correct in its estimate of value, the firm can repurchase stock at any price less than what management believes to be the intrinsic value without harming the financial position of those who do not sell. If management is incorrect (overly optimistic) and a smaller price/earnings ratio prevails, the extent to which the stockholders who do not sell are harmed is determined by the spread between the repurchase price and the market price.

Flexible Dividend

One real advantage of stock repurchase in lieu of cash dividends is that investors who do not want to convert their investments into cash do not sell their stock back to the corporation. By not selling they avoid realization of the capital gain, and they do not have any taxation on the increment to the value of their wealth (they also avoid transaction costs if they do not want cash).

The investors who want to receive cash sell a portion of their holdings, and even though they pay tax on their gains, this tax is apt to be less than if the cash distribution were taxed as ordinary income. By using stock repurchase as the means of the cash distribution, the company tends to direct the cash to those investors who want the cash and bypass the investors who do not need cash at the present time.

A Form of Dividend

Stock repurchase is a special type of dividend. If there were the same tax treatment for ordinary income and capital gains, and if a proportionate number of the shares are acquired from all stockholders, the economic effects would be almost identical for stock repurchase as for a cash dividend (the number of shares outstanding would change, and this would be the prime difference). The stock price would be different, depending on the form of the cash distribution.

If the stock is not acquired proportionately from all investors, stock repurchase is a special type of dividend, since it goes only to those stockholders preferring cash compared to increased ownership. Those stockholders preferring to increase their investment compared to receiving cash do not sell. The self-selectivity of the process is an advantage for the stockholders as a group. One disadvantage is that a stockholder wanting cash may incur some transaction costs (if the stock is repurchased in the market).

The foregoing conclusion assumes zero taxes. Once taxes are considered, stock repurchase has real tax advantages. The tax savings to stockholders of a stock repurchase compared to a cash dividend may be sizable. Suppose that an investor owns and sells stock for $1,200 that has a tax base of $1,000. The marginal tax rate for ordinary income is 39.6 percent and for capital gains is 20 percent. With a $1,200 cash dividend, the stockholder would pay a tax of $475.20 and would net out $724.80. With the $1,200 disbursed in the form of a stock repurchase the stockholder would net out $1,160 (the tax would be $40 on a capital gain of $200).

The advantage of repurchase over an ordinary dividend distribution occurs for three reasons. First, is the difference in the two tax rates. Normally capital gains are taxed at a lower rate than ordinary income. In the United States the maximum federal tax rate on ordinary income is .396 and the rate on the long-term capital gains is .20. Different tax rates are not the only reason for the difference. The second reason is that part of the proceeds from selling a stock is protected by the tax basis of the stock and not taxed at all. Although systematic repurchase over time would eventually drive the tax base to zero, the present value methodology weights the early tax savings high and so the difference between systematic repurchase and ordinary dividend is still consequential when both capital gains and ordinary income are taxed at the same rate. The third reason is that an investor by not selling avoids all taxation at the time of the repurchase. If both personal and corporate tax rates were zero, either method of income distribution would lead to the same intrinsic value.

The current tax laws provide powerful incentives for firms with liquid assets available for distribution to purchase shares rather than pay dividends. Under present federal and state tax structures, many persons prefer capital gains to ordinary income. The reason for their preference is that the marginal rate of state and federal taxation on ordinary income can be 39.6 percent while the rate on long-term capital gains is 20 percent.

Consider now a corporation with excess liquid assets that it desires to pay out in the form most attractive from its shareholders' point of view. If it distributes them as dividends, they will represent ordinary income to shareholders and will be taxed accordingly. If, on the other hand, the corporation buys back shares, a portion of its distribution will be regarded as a return to the shareholders' capital and will not be taxed at all, while that portion of the return that is taxed, namely, the capital gain, will be subject to a lower rate than ordinary income. In addition, the investors who merely want to reinvest are not taxed at all since they do not sell their stock.

Given these incentives for returning cash to stockholders by repurchasing shares, a relevant question would seem to be: Why do firms continue to pay dividends? Two reasons are that there are some investors who pay zero taxes and some stock is owned by corporations. A third explanation is that old habits are hard to change.

The current Internal Revenue Code clearly seeks to prohibit firms from disguising dividends in the form of share repurchases. Proportional repurchases, for example, are treated the same as dividends for tax purposes.

Examples: Price Equals Tax Basis
t_p =   Tax rate on ordinary income = .396
t_g =   Tax rate on capital gains = .20
P_0 =   Stock price = \$20 = Tax Basis
          The firm has 100,000 shares outstanding.

The investor owns .01 of shares or 1,000 shares.
The firm has $100,000 or $1 per share available for distribution.
It can buy 5,000 shares.

Cash Dividend
    Investor receives $1,000
    Tax (.396)   396
    Net $ 604

Share Repurchase of 5,000 Shares and Zero Capital Gains

The investor sells 50 shares and receives 50($20) = $1,000.
There are no capital gain taxes since the cash proceeds equal the tax basis of $20(50) = $1,000.
Would the investor prefer $1,000 from the share repurchase or $604 from the cash dividend? Clearly, $1,000 of share repurchase cash proceeds after-tax is better than $604 with a cash dividend. But the investor sold 50 shares. Does the sale of the 50 shares affect the conclusion?
Before the repurchase the investor owned .01 of the firm's stock. After the firm buys 5,000 of its shares there are 95,000 shares outstanding and the investor owns 950 or .01. With a cash dividend the investor owns .01 of the stock. The primary difference between the dividend and the share repurchase is that with share repurchase the investor has $396 more cash. A secondary difference is that the tax basis of the investment is $20,000 with a cash dividend and $19,000 after the share repurchase (a subsequent $1,000 investment would add $1,000 to the investor's tax basis.)
When tax considerations are included for a taxed individual investor share repurchase will beat a cash dividend.

Share Repurchase With a Capital Gains Tax

Now assume P = $40 and the Tax Basis = $10. There are again 100,000 shares outstanding and the investor owns 1,000 shares. The firm has $200,000 of cash available for distribution ($2 per share) and the firm could buy 5,000 shares with the $200,000.

Cash Dividend

Investor receives	$2,000
Tax (.396)	792
Net	$1,208

Share Repurchase of 5,000 Shares (Investor Sells 50 Shares)

Investor receives $40(50) =	$2,000
Tax: 50(40-10) .20	- 300
Net	$1,700

With share repurchase the investor selling 50 shares has $1,700 net of taxes compared to $1,208 with a $2 per share dividend. If the investor does not sell with share repurchase the investor will own1,000 shares worth $40 each or $40,000 in total. The selling investor has:

Stock: 950 x $40 =	38,000
Cash:	1,700
Total Value	$39,700

The decrease of $300 compared to holding the stock and not selling is the capital gains tax that must be paid. Share repurchase beats a cash dividend, but buy and hold beats selling the stock and realizing the taxable gain.

Example: Price Less Than Tax Basis (Investor Sells 50 Shares)

Now again assume the firm has 100,000 shares outstanding and $100,000 available for distribution. The stock price is $20 and the firm can buy 5,000 shares. The tax basis per share is $60.

Cash Dividend

With a cash dividend of $1 per share

Investor receives	$1,000
Tax (.396)	396
Net	$ 604

Share Repurchase of 5,000 Shares

The investor sells 50 shares and receives $1,000. Because the tax basis is $60(50) = $3,000 the capital tax loss is $2,000. Assume the tax rate is .396 for the loss and the value of the tax loss is .396 (2,000) = $792. The cash flow for the investor selling the 50 shares is:

$$\text{Cash Flow} = 1,000 + .396(2,000) = \$1,792.$$

If the value of the tax loss is .20 (2,000) = $400 we would have:

$$\text{Cash Flow} = 1,000 + .20(2,000) = \$1,400.$$

The cash flow from share repurchase is either $1,400 or $1,792 compared to $604 with a cash dividend.

Share repurchase offers very powerful tax advantages compared to a cash dividend assuming a .396 tax rate on ordinary income and a .20 tax rate on capital gains.

The Value To Be Added

Models have been developed showing the great power of share repurchase as a tax saver. For example see Bierman and West (1966). Assume that a firm has stable earnings (no growth) that it intends to distribute annually by repurchasing stock rather than paying cash dividends on the stock. For ease in determining the effects of the policy, we assume that all the present stockholders will sell a portion of their holdings to the company each period to keep their percentage ownership interest constant and that the firm declares a stock dividend each period to maintain a constant number of shares outstanding. The equation to follow assumes that the tax base at time zero is the initial repurchase price.

D = the annual cash distribution
P_o = the value of the common stock
t_g = the stockholders' capital gains tax rate
k_e = the require return of stockholders

The present value of the common stock is equal to the discounted after-tax cash flows accruing to the stockholders. After summing an infinite series and after simplification of a complex relationship, we obtain:

$$P_0 = \frac{D}{2}\left[\left(1 + \frac{4(1 + k_e - t_g)}{k_e^2}\right)^{\frac{1}{2}} - 1\right]$$

Example

D = $10,000,000 = annual cash distribution
k_e = .10 required return of stockholders
t_g = .20 = capital gains tax rate

$$P_0 = \frac{D}{2}\left[\left(1 + \frac{4(1 + .10 - .20)}{.10 \times .10}\right)^{1/2} - 1\right]$$

$$= \frac{\$10,000,000}{2}\left[\left(1 + \frac{4(.90)}{.01}\right)^{1/2} - 1\right]$$

$$= \$5,000,000\ [(361)^{1/2} - 1] = \$5,000,000\ [(19) - 1)]$$
$$= \$5,000,000\ (18)$$
$$= \$90,000,000$$

If cash dividends had been paid subject to an ordinary income tax rate of t_p = .396; we would have, using a basic dividend valuation model with zero growth:

$$P_0 = \frac{D(1 - t_p)}{k_e} = \frac{\$10,000,000 \times .604}{.10} = \$60,400,000$$

Thus the stock repurchase method of cash distribution will result in an intrinsic present value for common stock 49% in excess of that found using a cash dividend method of distribution, if the assumed tax rate differentials exist.

Dividends Versus Repurchases

The New York Times (June 23, 1995) reported a unique definition offered by Mark Usem, a Salomon strategist. He defined the relevant measure, to be compared to dividends, to be the dollar amount of shares issued minus the dollar amount of share repurchases. In 1994 companies sold $4.7 billion more of shares than they bought therefore Usem stated "We find no support for the notion that share repurchases have caused the S & P 500 dividend yield to be understated." This does not address the issue whether corporations are not increasing their dividends as fast, as they would if they were not engaged in huge share repurchases.

The Economist (October 7, 2000, pg. 89) went so far as to suggest that selling the stock might be a good idea when a firm repurchases "Whatever the lingo, when a company says buy, you should often think sell." The article suggested that many companies had overpaid for the stock they had bought. This is not surprising if the primary objective of the share repurchase is to give cash to its share-holders and repurchase is more desirable than cash dividends.

There is a large amount of confusion regarding the significance of share repurchases. *The NY Times* (October 28, 1998) reported that IBM had authorized an additional share repurchase of $3.5 billions of common shares. The president of Annex Research called the repurchase a "Wall Street perversion that benefits selling institutions to society's detriment and artificially inflates current earnings and growth." It is true that the earnings per share and stock price will both be higher with share repurchase than they would be with an equal cash dividend. IBM had previously reported a quarterly income of $1.49 billion. Thus the share repurchase program was consistent with corporate earnings and a reasonable level of corporate internal investment.

In 1998 General Motors Corp. increased its stock repurchase program by $4 billion ($9 billion of repurchases since January 1997.) *The NY Times* (February 10, 1998) reported GM's chief financial officer as stating "This actually returns capital to our shareholders more rapidly than would a dividend increase." Obviously, the CFO did not want to explain why share repurchases were more desirable than cash dividends. The reporter (Rebecca Blumenstein) was more forthright

"GM officials have signaled they prefer stock repurchases to dividend increases, partly because dividends are taxed twice, first as corporate income and then as individual income."

A Negative Point of View Towards Repurchases

Philip Coggan writing in the *Financial Times* (March 15, 1999) questions the extent of share repurchases "But might the passion for share buybacks have been carried too far?"… "This adds up to a recipe for disaster. But who will know when to call a halt to the buy-back craze?" Coggan does not question the sanity of a company increasing cash dividends.

The GE Announcement

Share repurchase plans that are announced signal different things to different people. Thus when General Electric announced a $10 billion share buyback *The Wall Street Journal* (November 20 1989, p. A3) headlined "General Electric Buy-Back Plan Signals New Tack, Reflects Earnings Optimism": As part of the announcement the company indicated a 15% increase in its quarterly common stock dividend.

Merrill Lynch

The Mid-Year 2000 Report to Shareholders of Merrill Lynch included the following (p. 2):

> ### Dividend Increases
> Merrill Lynch has increased its quarterly cash dividend 19% this year. On April 17, the dividend increased 11% to $0.30 per share and on July 18, the dividend was increased another 7% to $0.32 per share. The dividend has increased every year since 1991, and has grown more than four-fold over that period.

From 1998 to the year 2000 the firm did not have share repurchase program in order to comply with the requirements of pooling-of-interests accounting.

The dividend record of Merrill (the four-fold increase of dividends since 1991) makes it difficult for its corporate finance investment bankers to argue that any of its clients should reduce or eliminate its dividend as part of a corporate finance strategy.

The basic earnings per share for 1999 were $7.00 and the dividends were $1.05. The .85 retention rate indicates that Merrill is a growth company and yet it is selling its cash dividend growth to the stock market as well as its stock price growth. "The price of a Merrill Lynch common stock increased 25% last year and at a 30% compound annual rate over the last five calendar years." (p 25,. Merrill Lynch 1999 Annual Report.) What type of common stock investment does Merrill want to be?

McDonald's

McDonald's is a company that has decided that it is desirable to have a share repurchase program. In a 1986 announcement the company stated:

"The strength of our business and our growing cash flow allow us to increase share repurchase and accelerate expansion at the same time. We expect to accomplish our share repurchase objective while maintaining our current leverage ratios and strong equity base to support future global growth. We believe that share repurchase is presently one of the most effective methods of using our excess financial capacity for driving shareholder value within our current operating structure, and we remain committed to enhancing common stockholder returns."

But it wants to hedge its distribution policy by also increasing its cash dividend. In 1996 McDonald's increased its cash dividend from $.13 to $.14 per year. The dividend per share was increased each year after 1996 and was $.20 per share in the year 2000. With 1,359 million shares outstanding this $.20 per share dividend is an annual cash outlay of $270.8 million per year. Far less than the amount spent in share repurchase (a $3.5 billion three-year program), but still a significant dollar amount and the amount is growing.

I.B.M. (2000)

In November 2000 I.B.M. announced that it would increase its share repurchase program by $3.5 billion. It had bought back more that $14 billion of shares in the previous two years. The stock price rose $5.06 to $98.38 on the day of the repurchase announcement.

Toyota (2001)

In January 2001 the Toyota Motor Corporation announced it planned to spend $2.1 billion to repurchase 2% of its stock. This was the largest share repurchase ever undertaken by a Japanese corporation. The repurchase was encouraged by the Japanese government as a prop to stock prices that were declining as a result of a sell-off of stocks by banks and insurance companies.

Toyota's stock price immediately went up by 13%.

While it was expected that one result of the buyback would be an increase in the firm's return on equity (less equity on the balance sheet) we cannot be sure of the result since we do not know what return would have been earned if the funds were reinvested by Toyota.

Advantages of Share Repurchase Policy

The advantages of a share repurchase policy that are explored in this book arc:

a. the tax shield (tax basis) leads to more after-tax cash flow.
b. the lower long term capital gains tax rate compared to the maximum rate on ordinary income (.20 versus .396)
c. lower transaction costs for investors who do want to invest more in the firm (they do not sell.) The share repurchase is an "optional dividend."

d. the stock price through time will be higher than with a cash dividend (useful for managerial stock options.)
e. hides the dilution effect of issuing stock options
f. supports the stock price
g. the firm can take advantage of "unfairly" low stock prices (signals that management thinks the stock price is too low.)
h. the earnings per share effect can be positive

The primary disadvantages of a share repurchase policy are:
a. large transaction costs for the firm compared to retained earnings
b. lawsuits are possible if the execution seems to exploit insider information
c. signals no real investments (other signals may also be seen.)

A Split-Off

Assume a corporation wants to divest an operating unit so that it will become an independent corporation. One method of accomplishing the divestment is for the parent to split-off the subsidiary. Stockholders of the parent are given the choice of keeping the stock of the parent or exchanging the parent's stock for stock of the to be divested corporation.

One way to look at this transaction is that the stock equity and the assets of the parent are both decreased by the divestment. A second way to interpret the transaction is that the parent sold the assets and used the proceeds of the sale to buy its own stock. With this latter interpretation a split-off becomes part of a share repurchase process. The net result is a reduction of assets and a reduction of the parent's stock equity, the same as with a share repurchase.

Conclusions

We have shown that repurchasing shares can have a significant impact on the after-tax returns of stockholders. Should corporations that decide to repurchase shares be required to notify stockholders of their intentions? We have shown that the value of the firm's stock is a function of the form of its cash distribution. Thus it seems reasonable that shareholders should be advised of a company's distribution policy and of changes in that policy. The corporation that repurchases shares without giving its stockholders advance notice may be implicitly penalizing those investors who sell their shares without this information.

Corporations have offered many reasons for repurchasing their own common stock. We listed a number of reasons and then proceeded to examine each of those reasons in turn. Three factors are of prime importance: tax effects, transaction costs and the differences in expectations of the market and of the management.

It is very easy for a situation to develop where one group of stockholders benefits at the expense of another group; thus a stock repurchase program must be administered with care if it is desired to attain a position where all stockholders are treated fairly.

References

Bierman, H., Jr., *Corporate Financial Strategy and Decision Making to Increase Shareholders Value,* Frank J. Fabozzi Associates, New Hope, PA, 1999

Bierman, H., Jr., and R. West. "The Acquisition of Common Stock by the Corporate Issuer,"*Journal of Finance,* December 1966, pp. 687-696.

Cudd, M., R. Duggal and S. Sarkar, "Share Repurchase Motives and Stock Market Reaction," *Quarterly Journal of Business and Economics,* V35, n2, (Spring 1996) pp. 66-76

Dann, L.Y., "Common Stock Repurchases: An Analysis of Returns to Bondholders and Stockholders," *Journal of Financial Economics,* June 1981, 9, pp. 113-138.

Gay, G. O., J.R. Kale and T. H. Noe, "Dutch Auction Share Repurchases' *Economics,* V63, 249 (February 1996), pp. 57-80.

Grullon, G. and D. L. Ikenberry, "What Do We Know About Stock Repurchases?" f*Journal of Applied Corporate Finance* Vol. 13, N1, (Spring 2000), pp. 31-51.

Lie, E. and H.J. Lie, "The Role of Personal Taxes in Corporate Decisions: An Empirical Analyses of Share Repurchases and Dividends," *Journal of Financial Quantitative Analysis,* V34, n 4 (December 1999), pp. 533-552

Lucas, D. J. and R. L. McDonald, "Shareholder Heterogeneity, Adverse Selection and Payout Policy," *Journal of Financial and Quantitative Analysis,* V33, n2 (June 1998), pp. 233-253

Vermaelen, Theo "Common Stock Repurchases and Market Signaling: An Empirical Study," *Journal of Financial Economics.* June 1981, pp. 139-183

Chapter 4

Share Repurchase and Stock Price

What happens to a firm's stock price when the firm repurchases its shares? Initially, we will assume:

a.   the market price is equal to the stock's intrinsic value

b.   there are no psychological reactions by the stock market or signaling effects

c.   the market has anticipated the effects on stock value of a share repurchase program if such a program is to be implemented.

We will consider what happens to the stock price if there is a cash dividend and what happens to the stock price if there is a share repurchase.

Assume a firm with 1,000,000 shares outstanding and the stock price is $40. The firm earns a constant $4,000,000 per year and currently has $4,000,000 extra cash.

A Dividend

Assume the firm pays a $4,000,000 dividend ($4 per share) and there are zero investor taxes. After the dividend the stock price is $36.

$$P = \frac{36,000,000}{1,000,000} = \$36.$$

The $4 decrease in value reflects the $4 per share of cash distributed. If we considered the investors' tax status the decrease in value might be less than $4, but assume the marginal investor is not paying taxes and the $36 stock price is a reasonable estimate of the stock price after a $4 dividend.

Share Repurchase

Assume the firm can buy 100,000 shares with the $4,000,000 given a $40 initial stock price. The stock price after the repurchase, P_o, remains $40:

$$P_o = \frac{36,000,000}{900,000} = \$40.$$

The stock price is unchanged with the share repurchase given the assumptions. But, we have to consider the situation after one year and the firm has earned $4,000,000 during the year. With 100,000 shares repurchased at time zero, the stock price after one year (P_1) is $44.44.

$$P_1 = \frac{40,000,000}{900,000} = \$44.44.$$

It is shown in Appendix A that with no cash dividend and no growth in total earnings, that:

$$G = \frac{D}{V-D} = \frac{4}{40-4} = .111,$$

where

G   is the growth rate in the earnings per share
D   is the dollar amount of the share repurchase
V   is the initial market capitalization of the firm.

The stock price after one year will be:

$$P_1 = (1+G) P_o = 1.11 (40) = \$44.44.$$

The below table shows the progression through time of stock price, shares repurchased, and the remaining shares.

Time	Initial Price of Period (g = .111)	Shares Repurchased With $4,000,000	Remaining Shares
0	40.00	100,000	900,000
1	44.44	90,000	810,000
2	49.38	81,000	729,000
3	54.87	72,900	656,100

If the number of outstanding shares is too small or the stock price too large, the company can declare a stock dividend or a stock split to bring these measures to be consistent with the target measures.

The Growth Rate

The basic sustainable growth rate of total common stock earnings and earnings per share is:

$$g = rb + b\frac{B}{S}\left[r - (1-t)k\right]$$

where

r   is the return earned on new investment

b   is the retention rate

$\dfrac{B}{S}$ is the amount of debt used per dollar of common stock capital

t   is the corporate tax rate

k   is the interest rate cost of debt

If the company is repurchasing p of its outstanding shares then Appendix B shows that:

$$G = \frac{g+p}{1-p}$$

where G is the growth rate of earnings per share if the firm is repurchasing p of its stock and total earnings are growing at a rate g.

Example
     5 Shares outstanding with a stock price of $50

Total earnings $100
B/S = $2 ($2 of debt is issued for each $1 of stock equity added)
r = .15 (return earned on new investment)
(1-t) k = .05 (after tax cost of debt)
$6 dividend in total

$50 repurchase of one share $(p = \dfrac{1}{5} = .20)$

$b = .44$ or $100 - 6 - 50 = \$44$ and $b = \dfrac{44}{100} = .44$.

The sustainable growth rate of total earnings is:
$$g = .44 (.15) + 44 (2) [.15 - .05] = .066 + .088 = .154.$$

The second year's total earnings are expected to be:

$$EPS_2 = (1.154) 100 = \$115.40.$$

The expected increase in earnings is $15.40

		$100
Earnings		
Less: Dividend	$6	
Share Repurchase	50	- 56
Retention		$44
Earnings rate		x .15
Earnings from retention		$ 6.60
The firm issues $88 of debt		
The debt earns: 88(.15-.05)		+ 8.80
Total earnings increase		$15.40

The total earnings for year 2 are $115.40.

The earnings per share of the initial year are:

$$EPS = \dfrac{100}{5} = \$20.$$

The growth rate of the EPS is:

$$G = \dfrac{g+p}{1-p} = \dfrac{.154 + .20}{1 - .2} = .4425.$$

With a growth rate of .4425 the EPS of the second year is expected to be:

$$EPS = (1.4425)\,20 = \$28.85$$

or dividing the $115.40 of total earnings by the shares outstanding (4).

$$EPS = \frac{115.40}{4} = \$28.85.$$

Note that both g and G are affected by the amount of the share repurchase. Without share repurchase (or an analogous transaction) the growth rate of total earnings and the growth rate of EPS are always equal. There is no change in the number of outstanding shares.

When there is an increase in EPS and a growth rate is computed, the growth rate of the EPS will be a function of

a.   underlying economics of the firm (the r)
b.   the retention rate (b)

c.   the use of debt $\left(\dfrac{B}{S}\right)$

d.   the after-tax cost of debt ((1-t)k)
e.   the extent of the share repurchase activities (p).

There are three components of interest.
1.   the basic growth component (rb)
2.   the growth component contributed by the use of debt

$$\left(b\frac{B}{S}\left[r - (1-t)k\right]\right).$$

3.   the growth component contributed by the share repurchase activity (G-g).

For the example, we have:
1. $rb = .15(.44) = .066$

2. $b\dfrac{B}{S}\left[r - (1-t)k\right] = .44(2)(.15 - .05) = .088$

3. $G - g = .4425 - .1540 = .2885$
4.   The sum of the components is .4425.

The growth component of .2885 resulting from share repurchase activity is real. It results from the decision to do share repurchase.

Stock Price Less Than Intrinsic Value

Now assume the stock price is less than the intrinsic value of the stock. A share repurchase program will affect both the value of the ex-pected stock price and the intrinsic value of the stock.

Assume a firm has 1,000,000 common stock shares outstanding and that, management "knows" the intrinsic value is $80 per share and the market price is 50 percent of the intrinsic value or $40. The firm has $16,000,000 available to buy 400,000 shares (at $40 per share). After the repurchase the value of the firm is reduced from $40,000,000 to $24,000,000 and we have for the new share value:

$$\text{New Share Value} = \frac{40,000,000 - 16,000,000}{1,000,000 - 400,000} = \$40.$$

The share value based on market values is unchanged. The new intrinsic value per share is:

$$\text{New Intrinsic Value} = \frac{80,000,000 - 16,000,000}{600,000} = \$106.67.$$

The share value does not change given that the shares are repurchased at the initial market price. The intrinsic value goes up from $80 to $106.67 given that the stock is purchased at a bargain price (at a price less than intrinsic value). The ratio of intrinsic value to market price was initially 2 and after the repurchase the ratio of intrinsic value to share value based on market value is:

$$\frac{\text{Intrinsic Value}}{\text{Share Value}} = \frac{106.67}{40} = 2.67.$$

If the market effectively again computes the appropriate market price based on .50 of intrinsic value, then the market price would increase to $53.35:

$$\text{New Market Price} = .5(106.67) = \$53.35.$$

This share repurchase offers the possibility of enhancing both the share ratio based on market price and the intrinsic value of a stock if the stock can be purchased at less than intrinsic value. In the long run we would expect the market price to converge to the intrinsic value which is now $106.67.

Of course, the determination of intrinsic value is difficult or impossible in the real world; thus the above example is illustrative rather than being an exact prescription for adding value to the common stock price of a firm. However, we can expect management to have an opinion regarding the intrinsic value of the firm's stock.

Stock Price Greater Than Intrinsic Value

Now assume the stock price is larger than the intrinsic value of the stock. Again, a firm has 1,000,000 common stock shares outstanding and that we know the intrinsic value is $80 per share and the market price is 50 percent larger than intrinsic value or $120. The firm has $24,000,000 available to buy 200,000 shares (at $120 per share). After the repurchase we have:

$$\text{New Share Value} = \frac{120,000,000 - 24,000,000}{1,000,000 - 200,000} = \$120.$$

The share value based on market value is unchanged. The new intrinsic value per share is:

$$\text{New Intrinsic Value} = \frac{80,000,000 - 24,000,000}{1,000,000 - 200,000} = \$70.$$

The intrinsic value is reduced because of the premium (compared to intrinsic value) paid for the stock.

If the market price is again 1.5 of intrinsic value, we have:

New Market Price = 70 (1.5) = $105

and the market price is reduced from $120 to $105. Thus, the expected market price is somewhere between $105 and $120 depending on how the market sets the stock price. Of course, in the long run we would expect the market price to converge to the intrinsic value which is now $70.

Share Intrinsic Value Larger Than The Stock Price: Conclusions

If the stock intrinsic value is larger than stock price we add one more reason for share repurchase. The stock intrinsic value per share will go up as a result of the share repurchase. Unless there is a convergence of stock price towards the stock intrinsic value, the stock price may remain unchanged.

If the firm has desirable real investments we do not know whether repurchase is more desirable than real investments even if the stock intrinsic value is larger than the stock price.

Two or more sets of stock prices must be compared. The prices at both time zero and at future time periods for share repurchase and for undertaking real investments must be compared. Hopefully the prices for all time periods for one of the two alternatives will be larger than the stock prices for the other alternatives. If there are one or more time periods when prices are not larger, then these is not a clear preference for either alternative.

Stock Price Larger Than The Stock Intrinsic Value: Conclusions

If the stock price is larger than the stock intrinsic value, a comparison of share repurchase and cash dividends will still show the tax advantages of repurchase with high tax investors. In addition, even though the stock is over-valued the stock price after share repurchase will be higher than if a cash dividend is paid because the number of outstanding shares is reduced with share repurchase.

Losses From Repurchasing Shares

A firm can think it has a loss repurchasing shares if the stock price at time of purchase is higher than the price that was in effect when the firm launched the share repurchase program.

The firm can also think it has a loss if it buys the stock and then the stock price declines.

To protect against the first risk the firm can buy a call option. It can pay for the call (at least, partially) by selling puts. The selling of the puts, of course, introduces its own set of risks. A much better strategy would be to do nothing (do not cry over spilt milk.) Rejoice that the stock price has gone up rather than cry that the cost of each share purchased is higher than expected.

Has the firm suffered a loss if it buys stock at $12 and then the stock price declines to $10? There is no question that with the assistance of hindsight the firm knows it should have waited before buying the stock. It could have protected the decision to buy at $12 by buying puts with an exercise price of $12. Unfortunately, the purchase of the puts has a cost. Also, the market would not be enthusiastic about the stock of a firm that has bought puts on its own shares.

Any attempt to reduce the risks of a share repurchase by the sale or purchase of stock derivatives is going to have costs. Given that a share repurchase is primarily a method of distributing cash to a firm's shareholders, it is neither necessary or desirable to hedge the share repurchase transaction.

EPS Targets and Share Repurchases

It is important for corporations to reach the EPS targets set by the consensus of financial analysts. If a firm's actual EPS is less than the consensus EPS the stock market is likely to punish the firm's stock price.

Assume a firm with 1,000,000 shares outstanding (price of a share is $6) expects to earn $.98 per share when the EPS target has been set at $1.00. The first thing that is likely to enter a CFO's mind is to accelerate revenues or delay expenses. Assume that all feasible ethical actions have already been done. Now what should the firm do?

Assume the firm issues $3,000,000 of debt paying .06 interest. The corporate tax rate is .35. With a year's interest (the interest paid could be less) new earnings are:

Initial earnings		$980,000
Interest	$180,000	
Tax Saving	- 63,000	117,000
New Net Income		$863,000

The firm uses the $3,000,000 to buy 500,000 shares at a price of $6 per share. The new EPS is:

$$\text{New EPS} = \frac{863,000}{1,000,000 - 500,000} = \$1.726$$

The strategy illustrated by the example dramatically increases the EPS. The same type of change can be achieved by using excess cash or a smaller amount of debt. Also, the effect is likely to be larger since the interest paid is likely to be for less than one year. Using the above assumptions the new stock value per share is $8.10 (see Appendix C to this chapter):

$$\text{New Stock Value} = \left[\frac{V_u - B(1-t)}{V_u - B} \right] P_o$$

$$= \frac{6,000,000 - 1,950,000}{6,000,000 - 3,000,000} (6) = \$8.10.$$

ZYPS and Share Repurchase *

Lehman Brothers developed a security called Zero Yield Puttable Securities (ZYPS) that was issued in 1999 by Bank Austria.

---

* ZYPS is a service mark owned by Lehman Brothers, Inc.

The bond was convertible into common stock and because of the conversion characteristic the Bank was able to issue the security at par to pay zero interest. At the end of year 2 the investor could put the bond back to the issuer at par.

When Bank Austria issued its ZYPS its common stock was selling for $52.50 per share. Each bond was convertible into 15.873 shares.

Assume the Bank uses the $1,000 proceeds from the issuance of a bond to buy $\dfrac{1,000}{52.50} = 19.05$ shares.

If the bond is converted into common stock when the bond matures, the Bank will have a net reduction in number of outstanding shares of 3.177 shares.

19.050	Shares repurchased at time zero
15.873	Shares issued at maturity
3.177	Net reduction in number of shares

In addition to the reduction in the number of shares, the firm saved the cash dividend on 19.05 shares for each year from share repurchase until bond maturity.

What is the downside for the Bank? The investor has a put and can put the bond to the Bank and receive $1,000. The Bank could call the bond after the end of year 3 at the bond's face value ($1,000).

Since the bond was issued at face value and paid no cash interest, the Bank had zero tax deductions as a result of issuing the bond. It was expected that the investor would not be taxed until the investor sold the bond or stock and had a gain or loss, but this taxation would depend on the tax laws of the jurisdiction in which the investor resided.

A ZYPS could be defined to be a discount bond with a call option. The discount bond could logically accrue interest through time. The call option would lose value as the time till maturity became shorter.

Based on the put-call parity the ZYPS could equally well be defined to be the issuance of a stock with a put.[1] It is far from obvious that one should accrue interest on the stock issuance. Thus with this latter interpretation no interest expense (for the Bank) or interest income (for the investor) would be accrued. The repurchase of shares financed by a non-interest paying convertible bond is an interesting concept. By adjusting the conversion premium and the put some investors can be enticed to buy the bond if the stock price is expected to have a large enough variance during the bond's life.

Repurchases Financed by Debt to Increase Value

Stock value will tend to increase if the share repurchase is financed by incremental debt. If with a corporate tax rate of t the value of tB is added to the firm value when B of debt is issued and the proceeds are used to repurchase B of stock, then the stock price will increase.

Appendix C shows that the new stock value is:

$$\text{New Stock Value} = \left[\frac{V_u - B(1-t)}{V_u - B} \right] P_0$$

where V_u is the initial market capitalization.

<u>Example</u>
$V_u = \$1,000,000$, $B = \$600,000$, $t = .35$
$N = 200,000$ shares, $P_o = \$5$, $(1-t)B = \$390,000$
When \$600,000 of debt proceeds are used to repurchase 120,000 shares at a \$5 price we have:

$$\text{New Stock Value} = \frac{1,000,000 - 390,000}{1,000,000 - 600,000}(5) = \$7.625.$$

The value added to the firm by the \$600,000 debt substitution is \$210,000. The new value of the stock is:

---

[1]This was pointed out in a Johnson School class by Bill Weld

$$S = V_L - B$$
$$S = 1,000,000 + 210,000 - 600,000 = \$610,000.$$

and

$$V_L = 1,000,000 + 210,000 = \$1,210,000.$$

The value per share (80,000 shares outstanding) is also the value of the stock ($610,000) divided by 80,000 shares:

$$\text{New Stock Value} = \frac{610,000}{80,000} = \$7.625.$$

As long as we assume the value added to the firm from substituting debt for stock is tB and if the stock can be purchased at market price, the new stock value will be larger than the stock value before debt issuance and share repurchase. While it is the debt issuance that causes the initial stock value change, the reduction in the number of shares will result in stock value per share increases through time.

Repurchases Financed With Debt

Share repurchases financed by debt are not unusual. Thus *The Wall Street Journal* (February 22, 1999) reported "And many companies using debt are also announcing buybacks."

The article quotes the chief investment strategist at Merrill Lynch describing share repurchase as "a price earnings management scheme."

Methods of Share Repurchase

There are several different methods available to a corporation to accomplish a share repurchase.

The corporation can tender for a given number of shares. The tender may be for a fixed price set at somewhat above the most recent market price. The corporation wants a reasonable probability of the tender being successful so the margin above the most recent market price should be large enough to attract the interest of some investors.

A second type of tender is for the corporation to conduct a Dutch Auction for its shares. The investor indicates for four or five different prices how many shares are being tendered (a minimum number to be tendered at each price by an investor is specified) by the investor. The company sets the lowest price at which it will buy the number of shares it has specified will be bought. All shares purchased will be paid the same price even if the shares were tendered at a lower price.

A third method is for the corporation to buy the shares in the open market and to pay the market price. A broker will do the actual purchases. If the corporation wants to buy the shares later but at today's price, the company can use a hedging strategy.

In 1997 the Ethyl Corporation offered to purchase for cash up to 35,000,000 of its common stock at a purchase price not in excess of $9.25 and not less than $7.75 per share. This was a "Dutch Auction."

There are SEC restrictions on when companies can buy their own shares. They cannot repurchase stock during the last half-hour of the trading day or make the first trade for the day's trade or when the market resumes after a trading suspension.

Price Change With a Dividend and Taxes

Assume there are no investor taxes and a stock has a price of $40 per share. The day after a $2 dividend with the market not changing its level, the stock should sell "ex dividend" at $38. But now assume a tax rate on ordinary income t_p of .396 so that the investor will net $1.208 from the $2 dividend.

$$(1-.396) \, 2 = \$1.208.$$

The stock price, ex dividend, should be $38.792.

Now assume the investor sells immediately after the stock goes ex dividend so that the investor, taxed at .20 on capital gains t_g has a tax saving of .20 (P_0-P_1) where $P_0 = \$40$ is the initial price at which the stock sold before the dividend and $40 is also the tax basis of the stock. P_1 is the price after the stock is ex dividend. We now have:

$$40 = P_1 + 1.208 + .2\,(40\text{-}P_1)$$
$$0.792 = 8P_1$$
$$P_1 = \$38.49$$

It is shown in Appendix D that

$$P_0 - P_1 = \frac{D(1 - t_p)}{1 - t_g}$$

and if $t_p = t_g$ then

$$P_0 - P_1 = D$$

The stock price decrease is again equal to the dividend amount. Let $t_p = t_g = .396$, then

$$40 = P_1 + 1.208 + .396\,(40\text{-}P_1)$$
$$22.952 = .604\,P_1$$
$$P_1 = \$38$$

Selling Shares

Assume p fraction of the outstanding stock are purchased by the firm and that the investor sells p of the stock currently owned. Let

    N be total shares outstanding
    n be shares owned by investor
    pN be shares purchased by firm
    Initially investor owns:

$$\frac{n}{N} \text{ of firm}$$

After repurchase the investor who sells pn shares owns the following fraction of the firm.

$$\frac{n - pn}{N - pN} = \frac{n(1 - p)}{N(1 - p)} = \frac{n}{N}$$

The percentage ownership is unchanged by the selling of the shares.

Accounting Implications

A share repurchase program can under some accounting rules prevent the pooling of interest accounting method for a merger or acquisition. A discussion of the issue is complicated by the fact that the Financial Accounting Standards Board (U.S.A.) is well along towards issuing an accounting standard that would eliminate pooling of interests.

It is far from obvious why the decision to repurchase shares should affect the accounting for M & A activity. Let us hope the present accounting practice is modified, so that this restriction on share repurchase is eliminated.

Conclusions

In a situation where the market price is equal to the firm's intrinsic value (the most reasonable assumption) a share repurchase will lead to an unchanged stock price (if the market had already anticipated the repurchase), but this stock price will be larger than if a cash dividend had been paid of equal total amount. In the future, if the zero growth firm operates with unchanged total value, income, and share repurchase amount, the stock price will increase at an annual growth rate of

$$G = \frac{D}{V - D}$$

If the total earnings are increasing at a growth rate of g and the firm buys p proportion of outstanding shares that are repurchased we have:

$$G = \frac{g + p}{1 - p}.$$

Thus, stock price growth can be generated for a firm with zero real growth (g=o) using share repurchase. Ordinary income (from dividends) can be converted into capital gains taxed at a lower rate and these capital gains are optional, the timing of realization being determined by the investor.

Appendix A

We want to show that

$$G = \frac{D}{V - D}$$

Let P_o be initial stock price before any cash distribution

        V be initial firm value

        N be initial shares outstanding and $P_o = \dfrac{V}{N}$

        D be amount to be used for dividend

        P_1 be stock price after dividend or share repurchase

Assume V decreases by D when the cash distribution is made, but one year later the firm value is V.

Share Repurchase

Firm buys ΔN shares where $\Delta N = \dfrac{D}{P_o}$

$$P_1 = \frac{V}{N - \Delta N}$$

and

$$P_1 = (1+G)\, P_o$$

Since $P_o = \dfrac{V}{N}$

$$\frac{V}{N - \Delta N} = (1+G)\frac{V}{N}$$

$$G = \frac{\Delta N}{N - \Delta N}$$

But

$$\Delta N = \frac{D}{P_o} \text{ and } V = NP_o$$

$$G = \frac{\dfrac{D}{P_o}}{N - \dfrac{D}{P_o}} = \frac{D}{NP_o - D} = \frac{D}{V - D}$$

Appendix B

Derivation of

$$G = \frac{g + p}{1 - p}$$

where

G	is the growth rate of earnings per share
g	if the growth rate of total earnings
p	is the proportion of shares outstanding that are repurchased
E	is the initial earnings
E_2	is the earnings of the second year
N	is the initial number of shares outstanding

By definition the earnings per share (EPS) is:

$$EPS = \frac{E}{N}$$

After one year and the repurchase of pN shares

$$EPS_2 = \frac{E_2}{N - pN} = \frac{(1 + g)E}{N(1 - p)}$$

The growth rate of EPS (G) is:

$$G = \frac{EPS_2 - EPS}{EPS} = \frac{\dfrac{(1+g)E}{N(1-p)} - \dfrac{E}{N}}{\dfrac{E}{N}}$$

$$G = \frac{1+g}{1-p} - 1 = \frac{g+p}{1-p}.$$

Appendix C

Derivation of:

$$\text{New Stock Value} = \left[\frac{V_u - B(1-t)}{V_U - B} \right] P_0$$

where

V_U	is the initial market capitalization
B	is the amount of debt added and dollar amount of share repurchase
t	is the corporate tax rate
P_0	is the initial stock price
V_L	is the value of the firm after the debt is issued and share repurchased
S	is the value of the stock after the debt is issued
N	is the initial number of shares outstanding.

With no costs of financial distress

$$V_L = V_U + tB$$

Since $V_L = S + B$ we have

$$S = V_L - B = V_U - B(1-t)$$

The initial market capitalization is

$$V_U = P_0 N$$

The firm can buy $\dfrac{B}{P_o}$ shares so the new stock value is:

$$\text{New Stock Value} = \frac{S}{N - \dfrac{B}{P_o}} = \left[\frac{V_U - B(1-t)}{NP_o - B}\right]P_o$$

$$\text{New Stock Value} = \left[\frac{V_U - B(1-t)}{V_U - B}\right]P_o$$

Since

$\dfrac{V_U - B(1-t)}{V_U - B}$ is greater than one, the new stock value

per share is larger than P_o, the initial stock value.

Appendix D

Price Changes With Dividends

Determining the P_o-P, relationship.

Assume capital gains are taxed at t_g and ordinary income at t_p.

Assume the investor sells at a price of P_1, immediately after a dividend of D and has a capital loss of $(P_o - P_1)$.

Then $P_o = P_1 + D(1\text{-}t_p) + t_g (P_o\text{-}P_1)_p$

Solving for P_o-P_1 we obtain:

$$P_o\text{-}P_1 = \frac{D(1 - t_p)}{1 - t_g}.$$

References

Ikenbury, D., J. Lakonishok, and T. Vermaelen, "Market Underreacting to Open Market Share Repurchases," *Journal of Financial Economics*, V39, N2-3 (October, 199) pp 181-208.

Chapter 5

Choosing Between Real Investments and Share Repurchase

The Investor Perspective (Using Returns)

Appendix A of this chapter shows that retention (and investment) by the corporation is better than share repurchase, from the perspective of the investor, if the corporation earns a higher return (r, after corporate income tax) than the investor earns (r_p, after investor tax). This calculation requires that an estimate be made of the after tax return available to the investor. The investor is taxed at the same rate with an immediate cash distribution or a distribution in the future.

Example

$r = .10$, $r_p = .08$, $t_g = .20$, horizon = 5 years. Since r is greater than r_p, we expect that retention is more desirable than repurchase. If the firm has $100 of investment earning .10 for five years with retention and then the investor has a capital gain taxed at .20, the investor will have:

$$100(1.10)^5 (1-.2) = \$128.84$$

With the firm doing a share repurchase at time zero and then the investor earns .08 in the market, after five years the investor will have:

$$(1-.2)100 (1.08)^5 = \$117.55$$

The retention alternative is better than share repurchase since the investor can only earn .08 (after tax) while the corporation can earn .10 after corporate tax but before investor tax.

If the investor can earn .10 after investor tax, there will be indifference between repurchase and retention. But it is reasonable to assume that average corporations willing to invest in other corporations can earn more before investor tax than the investor can earn, after investor taxes investing in the same corporations.

The above analysis does not consider when the firm's low stock price creates a situation where the investor can earn an excess return by the corporation repurchasing shares.

Investment or Share Repurchase: The Corporate Perspective Using the Free Cash Flow Multiplier

We want to consider whether the return from using the free cash flow for share repurchase is larger than the return available to the firm from investing the cash flows in real investments. Appendix B shows the return from repurchase is:

$$\text{Repurchase Return} = \frac{1}{M-1}$$

where M is the free cash flow multiplier (ratio of current stock price to the free cash flow.) Define free cash flow for this purpose to be the cash flow from operations minus the capital expenditures necessary to maintain the current level of cash flows. Free cash flow can be defined differently if it is to be used for other purposes.

Example

The investor can earn .25 in the capital market. Assume a firm has 1,000,000 shares outstanding and a market price of $100. It has $20,000,000 of excess cash (free cash flow) and can use this excess cash to repurchase 200,000 shares. The $80,000,000 basic assets earn $20,000,000 of cash flow per year. Immediately after repurchase of 200,000 shares at time zero the expected market price is still $100.

$$P_o = \frac{100,000,000 - 20,000,000}{1,000,000 - 200,000} = \$100.$$

One year later the firm has earned $20,000,000 so that the firm value before the cash distribution is again $100,000,000. The stock price (P_1) is then:

$$P_1 = \frac{100,000,000}{800,000} = \$125.$$

The investor who does sell at time zero has $100 to invest (earning .25) and has $125 cash per share at time one and the investor who does not sell has stock that is worth $125 per share whereas at the beginning of the year the stock was worth $100. All stockholders can expect a .25 return from the share repurchase. To justify retention rather than share repurchase the firm must earn at least .25 on new real investments.

Defining P_0 to be the initial stock price and C to be the amount of free cash flow per share available for repurchase, then Appendix B shows that the price at time one P_1 may be computed using P_0 and C:

$$P_1 = \frac{P_0^2}{P_0 - C} = \frac{100^2}{100 - 20} = \$125.$$

The return from repurchase of shares (with zero cash dividends) using the basic definition of return on investment is

$$\text{Repurchase Return} = \frac{P_1 - P_0}{P_0} = \frac{125 - 100}{100} = .25$$

where P_0 is the stock price at time zero and P_1 is the stock price at time one. An alternative calculation uses the free cash flow multiplier M.

$$M = \frac{P_0}{C} = \frac{100}{20} = 5 \text{ and using the free cash flow multiple of 5:}$$

$$\text{Repurchase Return} = \frac{1}{M-1} = \frac{1}{5-1} = .25.$$

Assume the firm will earn $20 per share on its $80 basic investment (basic assets) and .15 on the incremental free cash flow investment of $20. The earnings will be $23 per share on the $100 per share investment. The investment return is:

$$\text{Investment Return} = \frac{23}{100} = .23$$

and this is inferior to the repurchase of stock return of .25. The .23 is a weighted average of the .25 return on the $80 base investment and the .15 return on the $20 incremental investment. The $20 incremental investment earning .15 is not acceptable given that the firm can earn .25 by repurchasing its own stock.

$$r = .25 \left(\frac{80}{100} \right) + .15 \left(\frac{20}{100} \right) = .20 + .03 = .23.$$

If incremental free cash flow investments earned .25 the investor would be indifferent between new real investments and share repurchase. The .15 return is inadequate given the .25 opportunity cost possible with share repurchase. This unconditional conclusion requires that the riskiness of the incremental investment is at least as large as the firm's risk.

If the firm invests the $20,000,000 of cash flow and earns .15 or $3,000,000 on the incremental investment and $20,000,000 return on $80,000,000 of basic assets, at time one the firm would have a value of $123,000,000. With share repurchase the firm value at time zero is $80,000,000 and at time one is $100,000,000 (reflecting $20,000,000 of earnings and $80,000,000 of basic investment), and in addition with share repurchase the investors have $23,000,000 of cash. Now assume the investors can only earn .15 after-tax on $20,000,000 of invested funds obtained from the repurchase. The .15 is equal to the return the firm earns on incremental real investments. In total, the investors have $123,000,000 at time one with either real investment or share repurchase if the investors sell at time zero. There is indifference in total for the investors who sell at time zero. But consider the investors who do not sell at time zero. At time one they have with share repurchase:

$$\frac{100,000,000}{800,000} = \$125 \text{ per share}$$

and this is larger than the $123 per share value with real investment and
no share repurchase:

$$\frac{123,000,000}{1,000,000} = \$123 \text{ per share.}$$

The investors who sell at time one and the investors who do not
sell will prefer that the firm repurchase shares rather than invest in real
assets earning less than .25. The $20,000,000 investment by the firm
earning .15 is not acceptable, given the firm's ability to repurchase its
own stock.

An Equilibrium Stock Price

If the market expects the firm's value to be $123,000,000 at
time one with the incremental real investment earnings .15 and the
basic investment earning .25, the firm's present value at time zero
would be $106,957,000 with a .15 cost of equity capital:

$$\frac{123,000,000}{1.15} = \$106,957,000$$

With the revised time zero price of $106.957 per share
(increased from $100) the investors who sell at time zero and who sell
at time one do equally well.

Sell 100 shares at time zero (investors can earn .15)

$$100 (106.957) (1.15) = \$12,300$$

Sell 100 shares at time one (firm has a $123,000,000 value):

$$\frac{123,000,000}{1,000,000} (100) = \$12,300$$

With the revised stock value at time zero the value of M changes to 5.34785

$$M = \frac{P_0}{C} = \frac{106.957}{20} = 5.34785$$

The firm's required return is now:

$$\text{Repurchase Return} = \frac{1}{M-1} = \frac{1}{4.34785} = .23$$

The .23 return now establishes the return that marginal investments of the firm must earn. If the basic investments earn .25 and the incremental investments earn .15, the incremental investment is not acceptable. If the incremental investment is expected to earn .24 it would now be acceptable whereas it would not be acceptable when the stock value was only $100,000,000. The desirability of share repurchase versus real investment changes as the firm's stock price changes.

Conclusion

A firm has the choice of investing in real assets or repurchasing shares. From the investor perspective the firm should invest in real assets if the return to be earned (r) is larger than the return the investor can earn after tax (r_p).

A second method of evaluating the choices is to define the repurchase return as

$$\text{Repurchase Return} = \frac{1}{M-1}$$

where $M = \frac{P_0}{C}$. This calculation of return makes use of the relationship of the current stock price (P_0) and the free cash flow C. As the ratio of P_0 to C decreases, the required return on marginal new investments goes up and funds should be shifted to share repurchase from real investments.

Appendix A

An Investor's Perspective

Is stock repurchase better than real investment?

Real Investment:

Let r_p = after tax earning rate of investor
   r = after tax corporate return on new investment
   t_g = the capital gains tax rate
   n = the time horizon

Assume the firm has $1 of cash and $1 of retained earnings. If the firm uses the $1 for stock repurchase (zero tax basis), after n years the $(1+r)^n(1-t_g)$. investor earning r_p each year nets after capital gains tax on the initial $1:

$$(1-t_g)(1+r_p)^n.$$

For $1 of real investment by the corporation (earning r) and then a capital gain for the investor the after-tax net for the investor is:

Is:

$$(1+r)^n > (1+r_p)^n \ ?$$

Taking the n'th root and subtracting one from both sides, is $r > r_p$? If yes, the firm should invest. For most corporations the value of r should (logically) be larger than r_p, for some investments since r_p is after the investor's tax.

  The cost of retained earnings equals r_p with either share repurchase (and capital gains taxes) or dividends (and ordinary income tax rates).

Appendix B

A Corporation's Perspective

Investment or Share Repurchase

Let V_1 be firm's total value at time 1
      N   be shares outstanding
      P_o be initial stock price
      C   be free cash flow per share at time 0
      r   be the average return expected to be earned on
             investment of P_o
      P_1 be stock price at time 1
      N_1 be shares outstanding after share repurchase of $\dfrac{NC}{P_o}$
             shares
      M   be free cash flow multiplier

<u>Investment of P_o</u>
      The firm value at time 1 is:

$$V_1 = N(1+r)P_o$$

and the stock price is at time one

$$P_1 = \frac{V_1}{N} = (1+r)P_o$$

<u>Example</u>
      C   = \$20, P_o = \$100, N = 1,000,000 shares, r = .10
      V_1 = N(1+r)P_o = 1,000,000(1.10) 100 = \$110,000,000

$$P_1 = \frac{V_1}{N} = \frac{110,000,000}{1,000,000} = \$110.$$

A .10 return on \$100 of initial investment leads to a \$110 stock price at time 1.

Share Repurchase

The firm can buy $\dfrac{NC}{P_o}$ shares.

The number of shares outstanding after the share repurchase is:

$$N_1 = N - \frac{NC}{P_o} = \frac{N(P_o - C)}{P_o}$$

And firm's value at time one with repurchase as time zero if the firm earns NC of cash flow during the year:

$$V_1 = (NP_o - NC) + NC = NP_o$$

The new stock price at time 1 is:

$$P_1 = \frac{NP_o}{\dfrac{N(P_o - C)}{P_o}} = \frac{P_o^2}{P_o - C}$$

<u>The Cash Flow Multiplier (M)</u>

Let $M = \dfrac{P_o}{C}$.

$$P_1 = \frac{P_o^2}{P_o - C} = \frac{P_o}{1 - \dfrac{C}{P_o}} = \frac{P_o}{1 - \dfrac{1}{M}} = \frac{MP_o}{M - 1}$$

The repurchase return $= \dfrac{P_1 - P_o}{P_o} = \dfrac{\dfrac{MP_o}{M-1} - P_o}{P_o} = \dfrac{M - M + 1}{M - 1} = \dfrac{1}{M - 1}$

A real investment must have an expected return greater than $\dfrac{1}{M-1}$ to be acceptable, assuming the riskiness of the real investment is the same as the firm's overall riskiness.

Chapter 6

The Return Earned By Share Repurchase

What return should an investor expect to earn by a firm implementing a share repurchase policy? If the choice is between a cash dividend and a share repurchase, then the return expected to be earned is not relevant. We do not compute the return earned by a cash dividend and need not compute the return expected to be earned by a stock repurchase program.

But with share repurchase there is an expenditure of cash by the firm and it can be that a share repurchase is substituting for a cash dividend and a future stock purchase. How should the return from share repurchase be computed?

The Expected Return From Repurchases

With share repurchase of one share there is an immediate cash outlay (P_0) and at the end of one year the company saves the cash dividend that would have been paid (Div) and the cash outlay necessary to buy one share at time one (P_1) to make the shares outstanding equivalent to the outstanding shares after share repurchase.

Define j to be the return earned by buying a share at a price of P_0 at time zero and we have:

$$P_0 (1+j) = P_1 + Div$$

$$j = \frac{P_1 + Div}{P_0} - 1$$

Example

$P_0 = \$40$, $P_1 = \$48$, Div = $2 where P_1 is the expected time one stock price and Div is the expected time one dividend.

$$j = \frac{48 + 2}{40} - 1 = 1.25 - 1 = .25.$$

Buying the share at time zero rather than at time one is expected to earn a return of .25. Since we do not know that the stock price at time one will be $48, we are computing an expected return using an expected price of $48 and an expected $2 dividend. The actual return is likely to differ significantly from the return based on the expectations.

The actual return calculation is the same as above but the values of P_1 and Div become the actual realized values rather than the expectations.

Undervalued Stock and Share Repurchase

What return does a firm earn by buying its own stock, if the stock is selling at a price less than intrinsic value? The first step is to determine the firm's value one year from time zero with and without internal investment.

Let

N	be the initial number of shares outstanding (100)
V_0	be the firm's total intrinsic value at time zero ($3,400) or $34 per share. The firm has excess cash at time zero ($400)
C	be the basic free cash flow per year ($300).
P_0	the stock price at time zero is $20 per share

Assume the $400 of excess cash is used to repurchase shares. With $400 of share repurchase of 20 shares (zero internal investment) at time zero, and with the firm earning $300 of basic free cash flow during the year, the firm's intrinsic value at time one is $3,300 before a cash distribution. The new stock intrinsic value per share at time one with 80 shares outstanding after the repurchase of 20 shares is:

$$\frac{3,300}{80} = \$41.25$$

The intrinsic value per share increased by the share repurchase from $34 per share to $41.25 (we shall see the intrinsic value is $37.40 if real investments earn .10).

If the stock price at time one is again $\dfrac{20}{34}$ of intrinsic value the new expected stock price is:

$$P_1 = \frac{20}{34}(41.25) = \$24.265.$$

If the value of P_1, is $24.265 the initial share repurchase at a price of $20 at time zero saves $24.265 of value at time one (a share repurchased at time one costs $24.265):

$$20(1+j) = \$24.265$$
$$j = .213.$$

The share repurchase gives a .213 return for the year to the remaining (not selling) shareholders.

Instead of a stock price of $24.265 at time one assume a stock price of $41.25 (equal to the intrinsic value per share). By the firm buying the stock for $20 at time zero the non-selling shareholders earn:

$$20(1+j) = \$41.25$$
$$j = 1.0625 \text{ or } 106.25\%.$$

The range of returns earned is .213 to 1.0625 depending on the assumed time one stock price that can be as low as $24.265 or as large as $41.25. For how long will the stock remain undervalued?

Internal Investment

Now assume that instead of a share repurchase the $400 of excess cash is invested by the firm internally at time zero and the $400 investment earns .10 or $40 in the next year. The firm's intrinsic value at time 1 is expected to be:

$$V_1 = 3,400 + 300 + 40 = \$3,740.$$

where $300 is the basic free cash flow on the $3,000 of initial intrinsic value and $40 is earned on the $400 of new additional investment.

The expected intrinsic value per share at time one is:

$$\frac{3,740}{100} = \$37.40$$

The non-selling stockholders have an increase in intrinsic value of .10 (from $34 to $37.40):

$$34 \, (1+j) = 37.40$$
$$j = .10$$

If the initial stock price is $20 and the stock price is still $\frac{20}{34}$ of the intrinsic value we have

$$P_1 = \frac{20}{34} \, (37.40) = \$22$$

The increase in stock market value is again .10

$$20 \, (1+j) = 22$$
$$j = .10$$

If the initial stock price is $20 and the stock price is $37.40 at time one (equal to the intrinsic value) the investors earn:

$$20(1+j) = 37.40$$
$$j = .87.$$

With these assumptions, share repurchase is more desirable than real investments earning .10. With share repurchase the stock intrinsic value can be increased to $41.25 per share (up from $37.40 with internal investments.) The stock price (assuming the same 20/34 ratio to value) increased to $24.265 (up from $22). We do not know when the gap between intrinsic value and market price will be eliminated.

Given the difficulty of estimating intrinsic value we cannot be sure that a gap exists.

A Closed Form Solution

It was shown in Appendix B to Chapter 5 that

$$r = \frac{1}{M-1}$$

where r is the return required on real investment to match the return from share repurchase. M is the ratio of the stock's market price to the firm's free cash flow.

Let M = 10 (consistent with the example if the firm did not have excess cash), then:

$$r = \frac{1}{10-1} = .1111$$

Real investment must earn .1111 to match the return from share repurchase. This relationship is valid only if the ratio of price to intrinsic value is not expected to change in the next year.

Purchase of Over-Valued Stock

The primary purpose of share repurchase is to be a mechanism for returning cash to a firm's shareholders. When the firm's stock is undervalued there may be other benefits (the return earned by the repurchase may be larger than alternative uses of the cash and the intrinsic value per share may be increased). When the firm's stock is overvalued the firm does not repurchase shares expecting to gain value from buying overvalued shares. However, we circle back to the fact that share repurchase beats a cash dividend if there are high tax investors, even if the stock purchased is greatly overvalued. The objective is to distribute cash to shareholders and this may be best achieved by share repurchase rather than a cash dividend.

While the corporation's choice of share repurchase over a cash dividend should not be deterred by an overvalued stock, the investor has to determine whether it is desirable to hold or sell. Obviously, in a situation where the value per share will be diluted by a share repurchase of over valued stock, the investor has to determine whether or not to sell.

Example
N   = 100, V_o = $3,300, the firm's intrinsic value at time zero or $33 per share.
NP_0 = $6,000, the firm's market value ($60 per share) at time zero. The firm has $300 of excess cash.
C   = $300, the firm's basic free cash flow per year.

With $300 of excess cash and a $60 stock price the firm buys 5 shares at time zero, and with the firm earning $300 of basic free cash flow during the year, the firm's intrinsic value at time one is $3,300 before a cash distribution $33 per share. The new intrinsic value per share at time one with 95 shares outstanding is:

$$\frac{3,300}{95} = \$34.74$$

At time zero after the share repurchase of $300 and a firm value of $3,000 the stock's intrinsic value becomes

$$\frac{3,000}{95} = \$31.58$$

down from $33 per share. The intrinsic value per share is decreased by share repurchase where the stock price exceeds the intrinsic value per share.

If the stock price is again $\frac{60}{33}$ of intrinsic value the new stock price at time zero after the share repurchase is:

$$\frac{60}{33}\left(\frac{3,000}{95}\right) = \$57.42$$

down from $60. To avoid losing $2.58 of stock value the shareholders might be willing to sell at a price of $60.

We can also reduce the $6,000 market capitalization by $300 and divide by 95 shares to obtain the pro-forma stock price after the repurchase of $300 of stock:

$$\frac{6,000 - 300}{95} = \$60$$

This calculation gives the same stock price after repurchase as before. But the calculation may be considered to be flawed since it ignores the shrinking intrinsic value. For example, if $3,300 of intrinsic value was used to repurchase 55 shares, replicating the above calculation we would obtain:

$$\frac{6,000 - 3,300}{45} = \$60$$

but in fact the firm would have zero assets having disbursed all $3,300 intrinsic value in acquiring shares immediately prior to the repurchase.

When the market price is larger than the firm's intrinsic value, a share repurchase at market price will lead to the investor having an incentive to sell some or all of the firm's shares immediately prior to the repurchase or during the repurchase.

Conclusions

A comparison of market price and intrinsic value is not relevant to the corporate decision-maker if the objective of the share repurchase is merely to replace a cash dividend that would otherwise be paid.

If the intrinsic value exceeds the market value, there is the likelihood that the non-selling shareholder will benefit by a value increment arising from the gap between market price and intrinsic value.

If the market price exceeds the intrinsic value of the stock, the share repurchase might still be desirable (in lieu of a cash dividend) but

the investor facing the prospect of value dilution has to consider the
desirability of selling shares.

Chapter 7

Share Repurchase and Earnings Per Share Buyback Parity

Management should not make decisions based solely on the effect on earnings per share (EPS) but the reality is that the effect of a decision on EPS does influence choices that businesses make. Will share repurchase increase the firm's earnings per share? Share repurchase will always increase EPS compared to an equal dollar amount of cash dividend. The interesting decision problem is to choose between share repurchase and real investments.

Appendix A shows that for a firm to be indifferent to a real investment and share repurchase, based on EPS, the real investment must earn:

$$r = \frac{EPS}{P_0 - Inv/N}$$

where:

   P_0 is the initial stock price
   Inv   is the dollars of real investment or of share repurchase
   N   is the firm's initial outstanding shares of stock

Example

Assume $N = 20$, EPS= $1, $P_0 = \$10$, Inv $= \$40$ and $\frac{Inv}{N} = \$2$. The value of r for indifference between share repurchase and real investment based on EPS is:

$$r = \frac{EPS}{P_0 - \frac{Inv}{N}}$$

$$r = \frac{1}{10 - 2} = \frac{1}{8} = .125.$$

This required return may be larger or smaller than the cost of equity capital.

With Share Repurchase

The EPS with share repurchase is the total earnings ($Y = \$20$) divided by the outstanding shares after repurchase. With the facts given the firm can repurchase 4 shares. The EPS with share repurchase is $1.25.

$$\text{EPS} = \frac{Y}{N - \dfrac{\text{Inv}}{P_o}} = \frac{20}{20 - 4} = \frac{20}{16} = \$1.25.$$

With Real Investment and r = .125

Now assume real investment rather than $40 of share repurchase. The firm's EPS with real investment of $40 earning .125 or $5 in total is:

$$\text{EPS} = \frac{20 + .125(40)}{20} = \frac{25}{20} = \$1.25.$$

With the given facts ($r = .125$ and the firm earning .125 on new investment) there is indifference between real investment and share repurchase. The limitation of focusing on EPS is that the above analysis does not consider the cost of equity capital. Assume the cost of equity capital is .15 and the best real investment for the firm yields .125 (consistent with above example). The firm should give the $40 of cash available for investment back to investors and share repurchase is the best method of achieving that objective. Just considering EPS does not necessarily lead to the correct choice from a value viewpoint.

If the $40 is returned to investors by means of a share repurchase process the $40 is expected to grow to $46 (a .15 return). If the $40 is invested to earn .125 or $5, the investor can receive $45 at the end of the year.

The firm repurchasing shares is more desirable than the firm investing the $40 in real investments even though the EPS is the same for both alternatives. Given that the $40 real investment earns only .125 when the cost of equity is .15 implies that this real investment is not desirable. The real investment has a negative net present value.

Assume the $40 is returned to shareholders by the share repurchase process and the $40 grows to $46 (a .15 return). At the end of one year with the firm earning $1.25 the stock is worth $11.25 per share or 11.25 x 16 = $180 in total. Stockholders have 46 +180 = $226 of value with share repurchase.

If the $40 is invested to earn .125 or $5 and if the basic investment of $160 earns $20, the investors total value is:

$$Total\ value = 160 + 20 + 45 = \$225$$

Buying the real investment is again less desirable than the firm repurchasing shares if the investors can earn .15 and the firm can only earn .125 on incremental investments.

Buyback Parity

From the viewpoint of maximizing EPS, is it desirable to finance a share repurchase with debt? Appendix B shows that EPS is increased if the earnings yield $\dfrac{EPS}{P_o}$ is larger than the after tax cost of debt. If $\dfrac{EPS}{P_o} > (1\text{-}t)k_i$ then share repurchase using debt is desirable for the shareholders based on EPS:

EPS   is earnings per share
P_o is common stock price before and after debt issuance
t   is the corporate tax rate
k_i is the cost of debt capital

88   Increasing Shareholder Value

Example
       Assume N = 1,000,000 and Total Income = $8,000,000 so that
EPS = $8;

$$P_o = \$100, t = .35, k_i = .10, \frac{EPS}{P_o} = .08, \text{ and } (1-t)k_i = .065.$$

If $50,000,000 of .10 debt is issued (500,000 shares purchased)
the after tax cost of interest is $3,250,000. The new EPS is:

$$EPS_1 = \frac{8,000,000 - 3,250,000}{1,000,000 - 500,000} = \frac{4,750,000}{500,000} = \$9.50$$

We have $\frac{EPS}{P_o} = .08$ is larger than $(1-t)k_i = .065$ and EPS is increased

by share repurchase from $8 to $9.50. The EPS increases since $\frac{EPS}{P_o}$ is

larger than $(1-t)k_i$.

The Break-even P/E Ratio

       For repurchase to be desirable (based on EPS) using debt to
finance the repurchase it is necessary that $\frac{EPS}{P_o}$ be larger than the after-

tax cost of the debt. Assume t = .35 then for repurchase to be desirable
we must have

k_I	EPS/P_o must be larger than$(1-t)k_i$:	P_o/E must be smaller than:
.06	.039	25.64
.08	.052	19.23
.10	.065	15.38
.12	.078	12.82

Example

$$k_i = .10, (1\text{-}t)k_i = .065, P_o = \$100, EPS = \$8 \quad \frac{EPS}{P_o} = \frac{8}{100} = .08$$

which is larger than .065.
    The P/E is:

$$\frac{P}{E} = \frac{100}{8} = 12.5 \text{ which is less than } \frac{1}{(1-t)k_i} = \frac{1}{.065} \text{ or } 15.38$$

thus, share repurchase is desirable (using EPS).

Buyback Parity and Security Analysis

Assume a corporation can borrow at a .10 cost before tax and .065 after tax. The EPS is \$1.30. We can rearrange the buyback parity equation to solve for the stock price (P_o):

$$\frac{EPS}{P_o} \geq (1-t)(k_i).$$

$$P_o \leq \frac{EPS}{(1-t)k_i}$$

Assume

$$P_o = \frac{EPS}{(1-t)k_i}$$

There is no premium or discount to payback parity if P_o equals $\frac{EPS}{(1-t)k_i}$. For the example we have:

$$P_o = \frac{1.30}{.065} = \$20$$

If the actual stock price is \$30 there would be a .50 premium to the buyback parity price.

$$\text{Buyback Parity Premium} = \frac{30-20}{20} = \frac{10}{20} = .50$$

If the actual stock price is $15 there would be a .25 discount to buyback parity

$$\frac{15-20}{20} = -.25$$

The larger the discount (or the smaller the premium), the more opportunity the firm has to enhance the EPS by doing a share repurchase financed by debt.

Conclusions

The choice between share repurchase and real investment should not be based on EPS but the effect on EPS is likely to be considered by management. The decision to make or not make real investments should be determined by whether the investment's IRR (internal rate of return) is larger than the appropriate cost of equity capital or better yet, whether the investment's net present value is positive.

In this chapter we have assumed the stock price before and after the debt issuance are the same.

Appendix A

Share Repurchase Versus Real Investments: Using EPS

Let:

Y	be total earnings
Inv	be dollars that will be used to purchase $\dfrac{Inv}{P_o}$ shares or for real investments
N	be outstanding share of stock
EPS	be earnings per share where EPS $= \dfrac{Y}{N}$
P_o	be stock price
r	be return earned on new investments

Share Repurchase

If the firm purchases its own shares with excess cash the EPS becomes:

$$EPS = \frac{Y}{N - \dfrac{Inv}{P_o}} = \frac{YP_o}{P_o N - Inv}$$

If the firm invests Inv in real investment and earns r the new EPS is:

$$EPS = \frac{Y + rInv}{N}$$

Solving for r

For the firm to be indifferent to real investment and share repurchase it is necessary that:

$$\frac{YP_0}{P_0 N - Inv} = \frac{Y + rInv}{N}$$

$$NYP_0 = NYP_0 - Y\,Inv + r\,Inv\,[P_0 N - Inv]$$

$$r\,Inv(P_0 N - Inv) = Y\,Inv$$

$$r = \frac{Y}{NP_0 - Inv}$$

or

$$r = \frac{Y/N}{P_0 - Inv/N} = \frac{EPS}{P_0 - Inv/N}$$

Appendix B

Buyback Parity

Share repurchase financed with debt. Repurchase is desirable (based on EPS) if:

$$\frac{EPS}{P_0} > (1\text{-}t)k_i.$$

That is,

Earnings Yield > After Tax Cost of Debt

k_i be the cost of debt

Y   be total common stock earnings

N   be number of common shares

$EPS = \dfrac{Y}{N}$ earnings per share

P_0 be common stock price before and after debt issuance

B   be amount of debt

t   be the corporate tax rate

With no debt the EPS is

$$EPS = \frac{Y}{N}.$$

With B of debt the firm can buy $\dfrac{B}{P_0}$ shares.

$$EPS_1 = \frac{Y - (1-t)k_i B}{N - \dfrac{B}{P_0}}.$$

Is $EPS_1 > EPS$?

$$\frac{Y - (1-t)k_i B}{N - \dfrac{B}{P_0}} \geq \frac{Y}{N}$$

Multiplying both sides by $N\left(N - \dfrac{B}{P_0}\right)$

$$YN - N(1-t)k_iB \geq YN - \frac{B}{P_o}Y$$

Simplifying:

$$Y \geq N(1-t)k_iP_o$$

Since $Y = N$ (EPS)

$$EPS \geq (1-t)k_iP_o$$

or

$$\frac{EPS}{P_o} > (1-t)k_i$$

EPS is increased if the earnings yield $\left(\dfrac{EPS}{P_o}\right)$ is larger than the after-tax cost of debt.

References

Kadlec, D., "Buyback Baloney," *Time,* October 2, 2000, p. 105.

Merrill Lynch, P. Caruso and D. Neviera, "Home Depot Buyback Parity Valuation Method Now Identifies More Feasible Risk/Reward Ratio," *Comment*, 24 February, 2000, pp 61-63.

Chapter 8

A Dividend Reduction Strategy

The CFO went to the firm's Board of Directors and suggested that the firm eliminate its dividend. The Board said it would be a signal that the firm was about to go bankrupt, and it was not an acceptable suggestion. The Board did accept a small dividend increase alternative. On the average a dividend decrease will be accompanied by a stock price decrease. But what if a firm's situation is not "average"?

It is conventional wisdom that a dividend reduction signals future weakness in the firm's earnings with the result that the stock price decreases after a dividend decrease. Normally, dividend decreases are accompanied by bad operating results and do forecast further bad results for the future.

Now consider a dividend reduction that is a result of a changed distribution strategy and not the result of unsatisfactory performance. To be executed successfully a dividend reduction should have as many of the following characteristics as feasible:

    a.   The reduction is made after one or more periods of increasing earnings.

    b.   The announcement of the dividend reduction should be accompanied by an announcement of a share repurchase program, possibly a cash tender offer for the stock.

    c.   The above announcements should be part of a public relations (and stockholders' relations) campaign that makes clear the optimism (justified) of management.

    d.   There should be an announcement of an exchange option where the shareholders can exchange their common stock that will have a low (or zero) dividend for a dividend paying preferred stock or a debenture bond.

The objective of the repurchase offer is to be fair to the shareholders who want a more reliable cash flow through time than the common stock dividend provides. By offering to buy the shares at some premium the firm gives these shareholders a reasonable alternative, the opportunity to receive cash and thus seek out a security more consistent with their financial objectives. The exchange offer suggestion is in the same spirit. Since the investors will be given an opportunity to exchange for a security that promises a larger cash flow, that is more secure, this results in more fairness than merely reducing the common stock dividend without giving the firm's investors choices.

The exchange for preferred stock can be organized as a corporate restructuring so that it is a tax-free exchange. The exchange into debt is very likely to be a taxable transaction. However, if a significant number of the shareholders purchased the common stock at prices that exceed the current market price there will not be a capital gain as long as the value of the bond received is less than the cost basis of the stock exchanged.

An Exchange Offer: Preferred Stock

Assume a company is presently paying a common stock dividend of $1 a year and the dividend is growing at .06 per year. With a .07 cost of equity and an assumption of .06 growth for perpetuity the value of the stock is $100.

$$PV = \frac{1}{.07 - .06} = \$100.$$

Some of the investors owning this common stock want cash flow and some want capital gains. The dividend yield is only .01. If the .06 annual growth continues, the following dividends will occur through time.

Year	Projected Dividend (g=.06)
1	$1.00
2	1.06
5	1.26
10	1.70
20	3.03
34.395	7.00

In year 34.395 the dividend will finally reach $7. Assume investors are offered a preferred stock that pays a $7 dividend in the coming year. The investors who exchange receive more cash than with the common stock for 34.395 years. If the market were to use the same .07 discount rate, the preferred's value is also $100:

$$\text{Value} = \frac{7}{.07} = \$100.$$

If the market were to use a lower discount rate, consistent with the lower risk of the preferred stock compared to the common stock, the preferred stock's value would exceed $100.

Assume the firm currently has 10,000,000 shares of common stock outstanding and is paying $10,000,000 of dividends. In order to conserve cash flow immediately, less than $\frac{10,000,000}{7} = 1,429,000$ shares would have to be exchanged into preferred (the firm could limit the exchange offer to 1,429,000 or less shares of preferred stock.)

Of course, after one year, with common stock outstanding paying a growing cash dividend the outlay would be

$$1.06(10,000,000) = \$10,600,000$$

If the high tax investors do not exchange they will save the tax on the dividend that they would otherwise have received. Assume high tax investors own 8,571,000 shares and they would have received dividends of $8,571,000 in the first year. The tax savings with the elimination of the dividend and with a .396 marginal tax rate are:

$$8,751,000 \,(.396) = \$3,394,000$$

and this tax saving increases through time.

If the zero tax investors owning 1,429,000 shares exchange their shares, the dividend that they receive increases from $1,429,000 with common stock to $10,000,000:

$$7(1,429,000) = \$10,000,000$$

Since this group of investors do not pay taxes there is no tax effect for them. The present value of the common dividends was $100 and the present value of the preferred stock dividends is at least $100, so the investors who exchange are receiving a reasonable deal. The high tax investors who do not exchange benefit from the tax savings with zero cash dividends and in addition the increased retained earnings in subsequent years will give rise to a more rapid growth rate for the corporation.

The exchange of common stock into preferred stock, if structured correctly, is not a taxable event.

Exchange Offer: Debt

Now assume there are two types of shareholders.

Type 1 own 40 shares and have a zero tax rate.
Type 2 own 60 shares and have a .396 tax rate.

The firm earns $100 before tax, has a .10 cost of equity, and a .35 corporate tax rate. The value per share is $6.50. The growth rate is zero.

The value for the zero tax investors (owning .4 of V_U) is:

$$.40 \, V_U = \frac{(1-.35)100}{.10}(.40) = \$260$$

or converting to a per share measure of value:

$$\frac{260}{40} = \$6.50 \text{ per share.}$$

For the type 2, shareholders (owning 60 shares) assume their discount rate is .0604 and the value is:

$$.60 \, V_U = \frac{(1-.35)(100)(.604)}{.0604}(.60) = \$390$$

or

$$\frac{390}{60} = \$6.50 \text{ per share}$$

The total firm value is 260 + 390 = $650 or $6.50 per share.

Now assume the common stockholders are offered $300 of a .09 debt valued at $7.50 a unit (40 shares may be exchanged). The debt pays .09(7.50) = $.675 per unit (the stock pays $.65 per share).

Assume that the value of the levered firm (V_L) is:

$$V_L = V_U + tB$$

where

t	is the corporate tax rate
B	is the amount of debt issued in substitution for the stock

Assume that 40 shares accept the offer to sell to the firm at $7.50 per share and $300 of debt is issued so that

$$V_L = 650 + .35 \,(300) = \$755$$

And the new value of the stock (60 shares) is:

$$S = 755 - 300 = \$455$$

or the value per share is:

$$\frac{455}{60} = \$7.58 \text{ per share.}$$

Assume the new cost of equity capital is .063, then we obtain S = $455.

$$S = \frac{.65(100 - 27)(.604)}{.063} = \$455$$

where

.65	is (1-corporate tax rate)
100	is EBIT
27	is interest paid on debt
.604	is (1 – investor tax rate)

.063   is the cost of equity capital with $300 of debt

The calculation of .063 is shown in Appendix A of the chapter.

Type 1 investors receive debt worth $7.50 in exchange for stock worth $6.50. Type 2 investors have their stock go up from $6.50 to $7.58. If we allow the corporation to retain earnings and for the investors to have capital gains taxed at the lower .20 rate, the value increment for type 2 investors would be even larger.

The above analysis assumed zero costs of financial distress and zero transaction costs. If these assumptions are deemed to be unrealistic the costs can readily be included but at a cost of increasing the complexity of the example.

The type 2 investors reject the bond exchange offer and keep their common stock since they compute the pro-forma EPS to be $.791, which is larger than the $.675 interest or the current EPS of $.65.

$$\text{EPS} = \frac{.65(100 - 27)}{60} = \$.791$$

Assuming the dividend on common stock is eliminated after the debt exchange, the $.791 would then be taxed at the .20 capital gains tax rate or less when the investors sell.

Empirical Results

Litzenberger (1984) states "with few exceptions, dividends cuts are made reluctantly by firms undergoing severe financial distress." Since few profitable and growing firms have historically reduced dividends we have the situation that a dividend cut signals financial distress. Litzenberger properly states "There is a great deal of empirical evidence consistent with dividend cuts signaling unfavorable information and having a negative impact on the company's stock price." We do not know whether the results would be different if a series of financially healthy firms reduced their dividends and the financial community learned that a dividend reduction did not signal financial distress for the firm.

But even with the conventional dividend policies in place, it is difficult to interpret the meaning of dividend changes. Thus in 1989 with many companies increasing their dividends Karen Slater of *The Wall Street Journal* reported (November 2, 1989, p C1) "Those dividend increases may signal trouble ahead for stock prices, some analysts warn" It also stated "... recent strong growth in dividends makes some market watchers anxious."

Florida Power and Light Company

In 1993 Florida Power and Light Company (FPL) paid $2.47 dividends per share. In 1994 it reduced its dividend per share to $1.88 (the dividend reduction was announced in May of 1994.) Earnings were $2.30 in 1993 and they increased to $2.91 in 1994. In 1995 the company repurchased $124 million of its stock and $69 million in 1994 (it repurchased zero of its stock in 1993.) From 1993 to 1995 cash dividends in total decreased from $461 million to $309 million.

The stock price ranged from $36 to $41 in 1993, $27 to $39 in 1994, and $34 to $47 in 1995. Certainly the stock price was not affected in a negative manner by the dividend decrease for very long.

CBS Corporation

In February 1998 the CBS Board of Directors voted to reduce its cash dividend to zero. The dividend per share had been $.20 for 1995, 1996, and 1997. The Board also announced at the same time a $1 billion share repurchase program. The Chairman of the Board stated "These actions reflect your Board's and management's confidence in the future outlook for CBS and our commitment to maximize shareholder value," (Letter to shareholders). The net income was $95 million in 1996 and $549 million in 1997.

The high stock price for 1997 was $32. In April 1998 the stock reached a price of $36. The stock recovered rapidly from any dividend reduction shock.

Aetna

Aetna decreased its cash dividend from $2.76 per share in 1995 to $1.29 in 1996. It purchased zero shares of its common stock in 1994 and 1995, but 1,194,400 shares were purchased in 1996. Net income increased from $250 million in 1995 to $626 million in 1996. The market price of the common stock was $69 at the year end of 1995 and $80 at the year end of 1996. The future difficulties of Aetna were not the result of the dividend reduction.

Sun Company

In June 1995 the Sun Company offered its common stockholders an opportunity to exchange 25,000,000 of their common stock for preference stock (a non-taxable transaction) paying $1.80 per share. The company also offered to purchase 6,400,000 shares in a Dutch Auction and announced they would also purchase shares of its common stock in the market. The dividend on the common stock was being reduced from $1.80 to $1.00 per share.

In 1994 the stock price had a high of $35. On the trading day prior to the offers the stock price was between $30 and $32. By the end of 1996 the stock sold for $24 and by the end of 1997 the stock was selling for $42. The dividend reduction was rapidly digested by the market.

General Electric

In December 1999 GE announced
   a. A three for one stock split
   b. A 17% dividend increase (from $.35 to $.41 per share per quarter)
   c. A $5 billion increase in its share repurchase (from $17 billion to $22 billion).

The day after the announcement GE's stock increased 2.9% (to $152). The 1999 annual report highlighted the following (p. 1) "The total return on a share of GE stock in 1999 was 54%."

PG & E Corporation

The dividends per share were $.49 a quarter or $1.96 per year. In the fourth quarter of 1996 the $.49 dividend rate was reduced to $.30 per quarter and in 1997 the total annual dividend was $1.20. Income available for common stock was $722 million in 1996, and $735 million in 1997. Total dividends were reduced from $844 million in 1997. There were no stock repurchases in 1996 or 1997 but in 1998 $1.6 billion of shares were repurchased.

In the first quarter of 1997 the stock price was $21. By the fourth quarter of 1998 both the high and low for the quarter were higher than $30. The dividend reduction did not harm the stock price beyond the immediate reaction.

Dividend Costs and Stock Price Changes

Rick Escherich, an analyst for J.P. Morgan (Economist, 1999, p.93) observed "that companies that trim their dividends still tend to see their share price drop by an average of 6%; those that suspend dividends altogether see prices drop by 25%." Of course, traditionally companies that suffered earnings declines or loss years cut or reduce their dividends, so a dividend cut was normally accompanied by bad earnings performance. Profitable and growing firms tended to increase dividends not decrease them.

Ultramar Diamond Shamrock (2001)

In February 2001 Ultramar announced it planned to repurchase $750 million of its shares (about 25% of its stock) in the coming months (within 90 days). At the same time the company announced a cut of its annual dividend from $1.10 to $.50 and an increase in its debt to capital ratio from 43% to 56%. The stock rose $1.33 to $35.13 on the day of the announcements. By April the company's price had risen to $39 in a down market.

The Decreased Propensity to Pay Dividends

In 1998 the percentage of U.S. companies paying dividends reached an all time low of 21% (see Fama and French, 1999). Less than 60% of the firms on the New York Stock exchange paid dividends in 1998.

Frequency of Payment

Traditionally common stock dividends were paid every quarter. This was logical when dividend were a large percentage of the investor's total return. Now that dividends are a decreasing percentage of the total return, companies are reviewing the issue of how frequently dividends should be paid. Baxter Corporation, Walt Disney Co. and McDonald's Corporation have all switched to an annual dividend payment schedule.

By holding the cash until the annual dividend is paid the corporation earns extra interest during the holding period. But the investor loses the use of the cash during the same time period, so the extra income earned by the corporation is not a real net gain to its stockholders.

However, there is a real gain in transaction costs. Sending out a dividend check each quarter is costly. The cost is particularly upsetting to management when the check is for a very small amount. By sending out an annual dividend check the cost of paying dividends is reduced by approximately $.75 per check.

A Dividend Capture Strategy

For years Japanese insurance companies were obligated by regulations to pay holders of whole life policies a return that must come from dividend income, not capital gains. To gain dividend income for a number of years in the 1980's these companies would buy high dividend paying stocks immediately before they paid a dividend and sold the stock immediately after they had legal rights to the dividend.

U.S. companies do the same type of transaction motivated by the 70% dividend received deduction. The U.S. tax law specifies a minimum time the stock must be held to qualify for the dividend exclusion.

U.S. individual stockholders paying at a high tax rate have an incentive to sell stock immediately before the date at which they receive dividends and translate the value added into a capital gain taxed at 20% rather than the 39.6% rate at which dividends are taxed. This strategy is facilitated by companies paying annual dividends rather than quarterly dividends. Obviously, the transaction costs would limit the strategy to investors owning large amounts of high yield stock. Most investors would conclude that the trouble of executing the strategy was larger than the taxes saved.

If the corporation issuing the dividend has a dividend reinvestment plan selling stock at a discount, investors have been known to buy the stock immediately before the dividend so that they can buy the stock at a discount. This is a form of dividend capture.

Conclusions

If dividends are to be reduced to zero (or close to zero) then the reduction should take place after good earnings reports, an announcement of a share repurchase program and a public relations campaign to explain the decision's logic. A final piece of the plan is to give shareholders an option to exchange into either preferred stock or debt.

The advantages of an exchange into preferred stock are that it can be structured into a non-taxable exchange and that the amount of stock equity is not reduced (nor the amount of debt increased).

An exchange offer into debt is likely to be taxable, but if the stock price has not been going up there could be a number of shareholders who would be taxed modestly or not at all. If the relationship for a levered firm

$$V_L = V_U + tB$$

is likely to hold (zero or low costs of financial distress) and if there is a proportion of the stockholders who pay zero or low taxes, there is a good chance that all investors will benefit from the exchange offer for debt.   The investors who exchange will receive a more valuable security.   The investors who do not exchange will have a common stock with a higher value.

Giving investors who want a current stream of cash flows, an option to continue such a stream (or even enhance it) is fair and should be considered by a firm that wishes to reduce its commitment to pay its current or forecasted level of dividends on common stock.

Investor's buy common stock for the expected growth.   But with a seasoned firm's stock the stock price reflects the expected growth, and an exchange into preferred stock or debt equal or greater in value than the common stock will also reflect the expected growth. The tax savings add value.

References

Benartzi, S., R.Michaely and R. H. Thaler, "Do Changes in Dividends Signal the Future or the Past?" *Journal of Finance*, v52 n3 (July 1997), pp 1007-1034

The Economist, November 20, 1999, p. 93.

Fama, E. F. and K. R. French, "Disappearing Dividends: Changing Firm Characteristics or Lower Propensity to Pay?" CRSP Working Paper No. 509 (1999).

Kalay, H and R. Michaely "Dividends and Taxes: A Re-Examination," *Financial Management*, Vol. 29, No. 2, Summer 2000, pp 55-75

Litzenberger, R. H., "On Dividends" *The New York Times*, Sunday, June 3, 1984 (letters to the editor)

Phillips, A. L., H. K. Baker and R. B. Edelman "The Market Reaction to Discontinuing Regular Stock Dividends," *Financial Review*, v. 32, n. 4 (November 1997), pp 801-819.

Slater, K., "Bigger Dividend Check May Not be Blessing It Appears To Be," *The Wall Street Journal*, November 2, 1989, C1 and C6.

Appendix A

Calculation of Cost of Equity Capital with Debt

Define the after investor tax cost of equity capital with leverage of L to be $(1-t_p) k_e(L)$, then if $(1-t_p) k_e(o) = .0604$, $(1-t) = .65$, $B = 300$, $S = 455$, and $(1-t_p) k_i = .05436$, then:

$$(1\text{-}t_p)\, k_e(L) \quad = \left(1 - t_p\right)k_e(0) + \frac{(1-t)B}{S}\left[k_e(0) - k_i\right]\left(1 - t_p\right)$$

$$= .0604 + \frac{.65(300)}{455}(.0604 - .05436)$$

$$= .0604 + .0026 = .063$$

where
$$(1\text{-}t_p)\, k_i = .604(.09) = .05436$$

Investors with a tax rate of .396 require an equity return of .063 after investor tax and $\dfrac{.063}{1-.396} = .1043$ before investor tax if the firm uses \$300 of debt. This assumes all after corporate tax earnings are paid as dividends.

Both sides of the above equation can be divided by $(1-t_p)$ and we have the more familiar:

$$k_e(L) = k_e(0) + \frac{(1-t)B}{S}\,[\,k_e(0) - k_i]$$

For the example, we have
$$k_e(L) \quad = .10 + \frac{.65(300)}{455}(.10 - .09)$$

$$= .10 + .0043 = .1043.$$

The .1043 is the cost of equity, before investor tax, if the firm has \$300 of debt and \$455 of equity.

We use t_p to compute the after tax equity return to illustrate the calculation. Other tax rates can be more appropriate.

Chapter 9

The Investor's Viewpoint

How should investors view a corporation's distribution policy? Obviously there are other considerations that affect whether or not an investor buys a firm's stock, but these other considerations are frequently difficult to value. The effect of distribution policy on an investor's wealth is relatively easy to determine and should influence a person's investment decisions.

Four Types of Distribution Policies

To simplify the exposition we will assume there are only four types of firms. A firm:
a. pays a dividend
b. does a share repurchase
c. does both a cash dividend and a share repurchase
d. does neither a cash dividend or a share repurchase (retains the earnings)

Firm Pays a Dividend

A firm that pays a dividend is attractive to tax exempt institutions and low or zero paying individuals. Even a person in a high tax rate bracket might buy a stock paying a dividend if the dividend is a small percentage of the stock price or the investor needs the stock for diversification purposes.

Hypothetically, a high tax rate investor could buy a high dividend yielding stock because the stock's total after tax return exceeds that of comparable risk stocks. But, normally we are not that confident that we know which stock will have a large total return, and thus the stock purchase should be influenced by the firm's distribution policy.

There are five problems with a firm paying cash dividends to a high tax rate investor:

1.   the investor is taxed now on the dividend
2.   the investor is taxed at the high ordinary income rate of .396.
3.   the investor wanting to invest will incur future investment transaction costs .
4.   the issuing corporation incurs costs of writing checks.
5.   the issuing corporation has the cash outlay of the cash dividend.

To reduce the costs of writing checks some companies pay an annual dividend rather than a quarterly dividend.

Firm Has a Share Repurchase Program

The fact that a firm has a share repurchase program is a positive factor for an investor. It is a tax efficient method of transferring cash from the firm to investors. The advantages to an investor of a share repurchase program are:

1.   investor is only taxed when stock is sold.
2.   investor is only taxed at a low capital gains rate.
3.   capital loss may result in an immediate tax saving.
4.   the stock price is higher after repurchase than it will be after a cash dividend.
5.   if the stock is not sold by the investor there is an increase in the investor's investment (proportion of the firm owned).
6.   the stock price increases through time (all things equal)

In addition, the firm's management who own stock options benefit from any stock price increases resulting from the share repurchase.

The stock price can be expected to increase, as a result of share repurchase, by

$$G = \frac{D}{V - D}$$

where D is the amount of the share repurchase and V is the firm's initial market capitalization.

Assume a firm has 1,000,000 shares outstanding and the stock is selling at $120 per share (V = $120,000,000). The firm has $20,000,000 from the year's earnings available for share repurchase. The growth rate in stock price in the next year is .20 if the firm again earns the $20,000,000 it spent on repurchase.

$$G = \frac{D}{V-D} = \frac{20}{120-20} = .20$$

After the repurchase and with the firm earning $20,000,000 the stock price can be expected to be $120 (1.20) = $144

Now assume a firm that is growing by .20 so that its stock price of $120 will grow to $144 in one year. Which firm is a better investment?

The first firm has an initial value of $\frac{\$120,000,000}{1,000,000}$ = $120 per share.

The $20,000,000 will buy 166,667 shares. When the firm again grows from $100,000,000 to $120,000,000 total value by earning $20,000,000, the new value per share is:

$$\frac{120,000,000}{833,333} = \$144.$$

A stockholder who bought the stock at $120 before the repurchase will have stock worth $144 if the firm continues to earn $20,000,000 (no real growth) per year.

Now consider the second firm. The firm is growing so that the total value grows .20 from $120,000,000 to $144,000,000. With 1,000,000 shares outstanding the value per share is $144, the same as with the first firm.

Which firm would you prefer to have bought stock in? As described, an investor should be indifferent. The investor starts with stock worth $120 and ends after one period with the stock worth $144 with either firm. If the investor sells the stock for $120 at the beginning of the year and earns .20 on the $120 this investor will also have $144 at the end of year.

If the second firm could grow in value from $120,000,000 to $144,000,000 and also spend $20,000,000 acquiring 166,667 shares at time zero it would be more valuable since it has growth opportunities that do not require the use of the firm's $20,000,000 of cash.

Firm Does a Cash Dividend and a Share Repurchase

Many firms pay cash dividends and at the same time have a share purchase reprogram. The dividend is attractive to low tax rate investors but unattractive to high tax rate investors. The share repurchase program is not an attraction for zero tax rate investors. The firm's attempt to please all types of investors is likely to displease (or not please) most thinking investors.

Retain the Earnings

Assume the firm can profitably invest all the cash flows from operations. A strategy of retaining the earnings is better than a cash dividend and is at least as good as a share repurchase assuming that at least some of the investors are taxed and there are transaction costs associated with raising new capital.

Calculations

Assume a firm has $100 available for distribution or rein-vestment. The firm can earn .12 (after corporate tax) on incremental investments and the investor can earn .07248 or .604 of .12 (after corporate tax) on incremental investments. The ordinary tax rate is .396 and the capital tax gains is .20. The investment horizon is 15 years.

Retention and then Capital Gain
$$100 (1.12)^{15} (1-.2) = \$438$$

Retention and then Dividend
$$100 (1.12)^{15} (1-.396) = \$331$$

Dividend and then Invest
$$(1-.396) 100 (1.07248)^{15} = \$173$$

Repurchase and then Invest
$$(1-.2) 100 (1.07248)^{15} = \$229$$

Repurchase, Reinvest in Corporation and then Capital Gain
$$(1-.2) 100 (1.10)^{15} (1-.2) + .2 (80) = 267 + 16 = \$283.$$

The retention beats the alternatives. Retention and then capital gain is the most desirable alternative.

While repurchase and then invest only has a value of $229, the investor who does not sell can achieve the same value as "retention and then capital gains."

The Psychology of Investing

Investors welcome evidence that the corporation in which they have purchased stock cares about the stockholders. Two methods of showing that it cares is for the corporation to pay a cash dividend or to repurchase shares. Thus while retained earnings may appear to be more desirable than either share repurchase or a cash dividend, the stock market might be awaiting a signal of support before it is willing to increase the firm's share price.

A Mixed Group of Investors

Unfortunately, all major corporations have a wide mix (from a tax viewpoint) of investors. Both pension funds (not taxed) and Bill Gates (a high tax individual) buy the stock of a typical corporation. This makes it difficult for a firm's Board of Directors to design a dividend policy. Either share repurchase or retention are sensible since most investors can meet their cash needs in a tax efficient manner with either method of distribution. Investors who want a steady cash flow without the complexity of having to sell shares to get the cash should seek high dividend payout firms or alternative securities.

A Stock Dividend

It is well known that a stock dividend (like a stock split) merely redescribes the ownership interest of a firm by changing the number of shares, but does not change the total value of all the firm's shares. There are those who think that a stock dividend might signal management's optimism regarding future earnings. There is agreement that a stock dividend could be used to reduce the stock price to a desired level (by increasing the outstanding shares and reducing the price per share). In this section we will consider a variation in the use of stock dividends so that their existence affects the cash flow to investors.

Citizens Utilities

In the 1990's Citizens Utilities declared a series of stock dividends. The company had two classes of common stock, A and B. Class A shares could be converted into Class B shares. Both classes of stock received stock dividends. Class B's stock dividends could be turned into cash at a cost of $.05 per share.

Class A shares could not logically sell at a discount to Class B shares since they could be converted into Class B shares. Class B shares could not sell at a discount since their stock dividend did not have to be converted into cash, unless the owner wanted cash.

Example
Assume there are 10,000,000 shares selling at $10 per share.
Market Capitalization = 10,000,000 share @ $10
= $100,000,000

Assume a 3% stock dividend (300,000 shares)

$$\text{New Price} = \frac{100,000,000}{13,300,000} = \$9.71.$$

The "value" of the stock dividend of 300,000 shares based on the new price and the incremental shares:

Stock Dividend "Value" = 9.71(300,000) = $2,913,000.

Of course, there is zero real value for the stock dividend since the firm's total value was $100,000,000 before the dividend and $100,000,000 after the dividend:

Firm Value After Stock Dividend = 9.71 (10,300,000) = $100,000,000.

Now assume a $2,913,000 cash dividend equal in dollar amount to the above stock dividend "value." Assume the firm's value decreases by $2,913,000 to $97,087,000. The new stock price is equal to $9.71, the same as with the stock dividend.

$$\text{New Stock Price With Cash Dividend} = \frac{97,087,000}{10,000,000} = \$9.71.$$

Appendix A shows that this equality of prices will always hold.
With retained earnings the new price is $10 equal to the old price (but the investor does not receive any cash).
The taxation differs for the three different methods of distribution being discussed. With a stock dividend there are no investor taxes. With a cash dividend there is income taxed at ordinary investor tax rates. With retained earnings there are no taxable incomes and no investor taxes.

But the owner of the B stock of Citizens Utilities receiving a stock dividend can ask for cash rather than more shares. Assume that .4 of the outstanding shares are B shares requesting cash, thus .4(2,913,000) = $1,165,000 of cash goes to B shares on the sale of the 120,000 stock dividend shares at a price of $9.71.

As a short-term capital gain the stock dividend converted into cash would be taxed at the investor's ordinary income tax rates. If the broker executed the sale, sold 120,000 shares held for over a year, then the capital gain would be taxed at the .2 long-term capital gains rate (unless the IRS rejected the practice).

One complexity arises when the investor choosing stock is to receive a fraction of a share as the result of the stock dividend and the company pays cash in lieu of the fractional share. Unfortunately, this receipt of cash is a taxable event, thus creating complexity for the investor. This problem can be solved by the firm keeping track of fractional shares rather than paying cash. An alternative solution would be to round off the shares to be awarded (if .5 or more of a share the investor gets a share otherwise the investor gets zero). Citizens Utilities has stopped the practice of issuing regular stock dividends. Probably there was too much complexity.

Conclusions

Stock dividends in lieu of cash dividends allow the investor to decide whether to receive additional shares of stock or to receive cash. While Citizens had two classes of stock, one class of stock, where the investor then decided whether or not to receive cash instead of additional shares, would be adequate. The two classes of stock were a residual of a past capital structure strategy.

The advantage of the stock dividend process is that the investor receiving the shares of stock is not taxed. The investor receiving the cash is taxed, but it is a capital gains (short or long). Admittedly, the tax situation is complex since the investor's tax basis per share will be revised after each transaction. The record keeping nuisance factor is likely to restrict the use of stock dividends with an option to convert the shares to cash. Most investors do not want this tax complexity.

It is interesting that the stock price after a stock dividend can be expected to be equal to the stock price after a cash dividend of equal "value".

A firm's distribution policy is an important factor for an investor to consider in forming a portfolio. The firm's distribution policy directly affects both the investor's cash flow and amount to be paid in taxes, thus affects the investor's future wealth.

Appendix A

The Price With Stock Dividends and Cash Dividends

We want to show that the ex post price is the same with a stock dividend and a cash dividend (the numbers of shares and total firm values are different).

Let   V   be initial firm value
           N   be number of outstanding shares
           p   be stock dividend (as a fraction of outstanding shares)
           Div   be value equivalent of stock dividend
           D   be cash dividend equal to Div
           P_1 be ex post stock price with stock dividend
           P*   be ex post stock price with cash dividend

With a stock dividend of p:

$$P_1 = \frac{V}{(1+p)N}$$

Define the "value" of the stock dividend to be:

$$\text{Stock Dividend "Value"} = \text{Div} = pN\,P_1$$

Substituting for P_1:

$$\text{Div} = pN\,\frac{V}{(1+p)N} = \frac{pV}{1+p}.$$

Assume the cash dividend, D = Div so that $D = \dfrac{pV}{1+p}$

$$P* = \frac{V - \dfrac{pV}{1+p}}{N} = \frac{(1+p)V - pV}{(1+p)N} = \frac{V}{(1+p)N}$$

Therefore, $P_1 = P*$. The firm's total value after a stock dividend is V (unchanged) and with a cash dividend is:

$$\left(V - \frac{pV}{1+p}\right) \text{ or (V-D)}$$

Chapter 10

Dividend Reinvestment Plans (DRIP's)

Start with the fact that many corporations pay cash dividends and that some of these same corporations need equity capital. From these facts evolved the popular dividend reinvestment plans (DRIP's) of dividend paying corporations.

The firm's common stock investors who sign up for the DRIP commit any cash dividend paid by the firm to be reinvested in the firm. A DRIP's obtaining of shares for distribution to the investors is implemented by corporations in two different ways. The firm can either issue new shares for the members of the DRIP and thus raise new capital or it can go to the market and buy the shares (thus support the firm's stock price.) In either case the stockholders participating in a DRIP have income equal to the dividend taxed at ordinary tax rates.

We will review the situation where the firm's DRIP issues new shares and thus raises new capital from some of its old shareholders. The corporation could have increased its equity capital by retaining earnings and the stockholder would not be taxed with this transaction. Thus for the investors increasing their investments the DRIP with the firm issuing new shares is beaten by retained earnings both by the tax effects and by transaction costs. However, if the firm is going to pay a cash dividend and if it needs equity capital a DRIP is likely to raise equity capital cheaper than the alternative ways of raising new capital.

A DRIP With Discount Stock Purchase

Some firms will allow their stockholders who are enrolled in its DRIP to buy the firm's stock at a discount and with reduced or no transaction costs. The objective is to attract more of its stockholders to join the plan than would be attracted with no discount.

Consider the common situation where a corporation is paying a cash dividend and has a dividend reinvestment plan that attracts individual (taxed) investors by allowing these investors to buy the firm's shares at a 5% discount from market price. Assume the firm's stock is selling at $100 and the company pays $95 of dividends to an investor owning 100 shares ($.95 per share.) The investor can receive $95 cash or a share of stock with a $100 market value (if the stock price does not change.)

In accordance with the U.S. tax law the investor has $100 of taxable income. With a strict interpretation of the tax law both the $95 of cash dividends and the $5 of discount are taxable as income. If all investors participate in the plan, the $5 of discount income is not real, but rather is analogous to a stock dividend. For example, if in the above situation the $100 stock price is before the dividend declaration and the firm has outstanding 1,000,000 shares and declares $950,000 of dividends, with all investors in the plan, there will be 10,000 new shares issued with the entire $950,000 reinvested. The firm value is unchanged, the number of shares increased by 10,000 and the new stock price is $\frac{100,000,000}{1,010,000}$ and the total stock value is still $100,000,000.

With a zero price discount and a $100 stock price there will be 9,500 new shares issued. The new stock price after the stock issue will be $\frac{100,000,000}{1,009,500}$ and the total stock value will again be $100,000,000. The price discount does not give value to the investor, merely added income taxes.

If some investors do not join the plan, there can be dilution of the non-joiners' ownership position. The investors who join the plan will have an increased ownership of the firm. If the firm's value is increased by the availability of capital raised at a lower cost than the alternative sources, it is possible that all the common stockholders are better off than if dividends were paid without a DRIP.

Zero or Negative Net Present Value Projects

The existence of positive net present value projects that would not be undertaken without the DRIP and a situation where the cost of raising the equity capital using alternative methods would be larger than with a DRIP help justify the giving of discounts to the participants of the DRIP. Obviously, the relative size of the discount and the present value of the cash flows obtained by the DRIP determine whether or not the positions of the non-participants are enhanced or harmed by the discount.

Continue the above example where the stock price is $100 and the firm has outstanding 1,000,000 shares. The dividend is $950,000 ($.95 per share) and half the shares belong to the DRIP which gives a 5% discount on the share purchase. Assuming a $475,000 cash dividend and $475,000 of zero NPV projects and 5,000 new shares issued for $475,000 of DRIP participation the new stock price is:

$$\text{New Stock Price} = \frac{100,000,000 - 475,000}{1,005,000} = \$99.03$$

The investors who owned 500,000 shares and purchased 5,000 shares (using the $450,000 of dividends) at $95 per share have a value of:

$$\text{Value} = 99.03\ (500,000) + 99.03\ (5,000) = \$50,010,000$$

The investors who owned 500,000 shares and received $475,000 of cash dividends have a value of:

$$\text{Value} = 99.03\ (500,000) + 475,000 = \$49,990,000$$

For this second group to be as well off as the investors in the DRIP, the stock price (P) after the dividend would have to be lowered to $95:

$$P\ (505,000) = P\ (500,000) + 475,000$$
$$P = \$95$$

With a stock price of $95 the firm's value (1,005,000 shares out-standing) is:

$$\text{Value} = 95\ (505,000) + 475,000 = \$47,975,000$$

The investors who received the $475,000 of cash dividends would have $475,000 of cash and 500,000 shares:

$$Value = 95 \ (500,000) = \$47,975,000.$$

The investors who were members of the DRIP would also have:

$$Value = 95(1,005,000) = \$95,475,000$$

For the firm to have a value of only $95,475,000 it would have to invest in projects with a negative NPV of $4,050,000.

$$Value = \$100,000,000 - 475,000 - 4,050,000 = \$95,475,000$$

Positive NPV Projects

Assume that with a DRIP and a 5% stock purchase discount the new stock price would be $99.03. How can the stock price again be $100? There are 1,005,000 shares outstanding. Assume the firm value is $100,500,000 and the stock price is $100.

$$New \ Stock \ Price \ = \ \frac{100,500,000}{1,005,000} = \$100$$

The investments financed by the retained earnings of $475,000 must have a NPV of $975,000 for the firm value to be $100,500,00.

Initial Firm Value	$100,000,000
Cash Dividend	- 475,000
	99,525,000
NPV	+ 975,000
New Firm Value	$100,500,000

Positive NPV Projects can cause the use of a DRIP to raise new equity capital to be more valuable than not raising the capital. With the above example a project with a NPV of more than $975,000 results in the use of a DRIP and undertaking the project to have more value than not increasing the equity capital and undertaking the project.

While the DRIP is used above to raise new equity capital it does not mean the stockholders who do not participate in the DRIP are better off than the stockholders who are part of the DRIP.

Stockholders Who Do Not Participate in DRIP

Consistent with the above example, the firm's value is $100,500,000 and there are 1,005,000 shares outstanding (the stock's value is $100 per share.) The stockholders who do not participate in the DRIP will have $475,000 of cash and 500,000 shares.

$$Value = 100 (500,000) + 475,000 = \$50,475.000$$

The stockholders who do participate have 505,000 shares.

$$Value = 100 (505,000) = \$50,500,000$$

The stockholders who participate are marginally better off than the investors who take the cash if the firm value is $100,500,000. Both types of investors are better off with the DRIP and the positive NPV investment than without the DRIP and the investment.

Fees of Raising Capital

Continuing the above example and zero NPV investments, the DRIP leads to a value of the firm of $99,525,000 and a value per share $99.03. The firm has "raised" $475,000 of capital at a cost of $75,000.

Now assume that without a DRIP the firm could have paid a $950,000 dividend and issued 5,000 shares and raised $475,000. The firm's value is:

$$Firm's\ value = 100,000,000 - 950,000 + 475,000 - 75,000$$
$$= \$99,450,000$$

and the value per share is: $\dfrac{99,450,00}{1,005,000}$ = $98.96

The $99.03 share value per share is larger with the DRIP than the $98.96 share price with the $75,000 finance cost associated with raising new capital in the market.

Conclusions

If we stretch our imagination, explanations for dividends can be generated. The easiest explanation is that the investors of a specific corporation are all exempt from taxes (e.g. pension funds) and need cash flow. Another explanation is that if stock repurchases were not legal, or were taxed at higher rates than cash dividends (as if a corporation owned the stock), again dividends could be justified.

A cash dividend for individual investors can also be defended using the argument that investors want cash from the corporation with the expending of a minimum of personal effort (a share repurchase would require selling shares and reporting a taxable capital gain.) When a corporation pays a cash dividend but has a dividend reinvestment plan where new shares are issued is not paying cash to the investor. The net result is a tax outlay by the investor that could have been avoided by the corporation retaining earnings.

While retained earnings are more desirable for investors than the corporation raising equity by the use of a DRIP, given a cash dividend the DRIP is likely to be a more desirable way of raising equity capital than the alternatives.

There are two different ways of evaluating dividend reinvestment plans with new shares issued. First, they can be compared to retained earnings. Retained earnings wins this comparison as long as there are investor taxes and transaction costs.

Secondly, if the corporation is going to pay a cash dividend when it needs capital, a dividend reinvestment plan may compare favorably on a cost basis with other ways of raising capital. Thus it may be that the corporation should not pay a cash dividend, but if it is paying a dividend, a dividend reinvestment plan is likely to be better than no plan.

References

Hagaman, T.C., "Raising Capital through DRP's", *Management Accounting*, September 1990, pp 14015

Scholes, M.S. and M.A. Wolfson, "Decentralized Investment Banking," *Journal of Financial Economics*, 23 (1889) pp 7-35

Stern, J., "Corporate Shell Game," *The Wall Street Journal*, November 13, 1978, p 23

Willis, A., "A Decade of Dividend Reinvestment," *Australian Accountant*, August 1989, pp 65-73

Chapter 11

Repurchase of Shares Accompanied by the Selling of Puts

Should a company that intends to repurchase stock concurrently sell puts on its stocks? As one chairman of the board incorrectly stated: "This is a no-brainer. The stock price will go up and this is easy money." We want to consider the pros and cons of the strategy of a firm selling puts on its own stock.

The Strategy

Assume a company intends to buy 1,000,000 of its shares. It wants to buy the stock at a price of $10. The stock is now selling at a price of $12. How can a $10 purchase price be achieved?

Assume the company buys the stock at $12 and sells1,000,000 puts for $2 a share with an exercise price of $11 and at maturity of the puts the stock is selling at more than $11. The net cost of the stock purchase is $10 per share.

$$\text{Net Cost} = 12 - 2 = \$10 \text{ per share}$$

The relevant fact is that $2,000,000 was obtained from the sale of the puts making the net cost of the stock repurchase $10,000,000 or $10 per share. Assume the stock price at the put's maturity is larger than $11. The net cost of the share repurchase is $10, the $12 price paid less the $2 per share received from the sale of the puts.

Of course, the sale of the puts means that the company must pay ($11-P) per share to the buyer of the puts if the stock price (P) is less than $11 at the maturity of the puts. For example, assume the stock price at maturity of the put is $6. The company pays $12 for the stock, receives $2 for the sale of the put for a net cost of $10 and pays $5 per share to the buyer of the put for a total cost of $15.

The stock could have been repurchased at a cost of $6,000,000 with no sales of puts and with the firm waiting until the stock price decreases to $6 to buy. The company paid an extra $9,000,000 if we include the cost of the puts as a cost of buying the stock.

The firm could buy the stock now for $12 per share and sell a put for $2 for a net cost of $10. But if the stock price is $6 at maturity of the put, the firm will have a put cost of $5. Thus the net cost of buying the stock and selling the put is $15. As long as the stock price at the put's maturity is less than $11 the cost of the stock purchase and selling the put will be larger than $10 if the stock can be purchased immediately at a $12 price and the put sold for $2.

Two Transactions

The repurchase of the stock is actually a separate transaction from the selling of the puts. A combination of the two transactions, with an assumption that the stock price at maturity will be larger than the exercise price, with probability one, is misleading.

Unfortunately when the stock price is lower than the put's exercise price is not a time when the firm wants an additional cash outlay associated with the put contract. It might prefer to use that cash to buy up the stock at the lower prices. If the decrease in stock price is the result of faltering performance the firm might want to use available cash to improve operations.

The Put-Call Parity

The put-call parity relationship allows us to analyze what is actually happening when the puts are sold. Let E be the exercise price of the put and the call and the face value of the bond. These three securities all mature on the same date. Then the basic put-call parity relationship is:

$$\text{Buy Stock} + \text{Buy Put} = \text{Buy Bond} + \text{Buy Call}$$

or changing this equation to facilitate our analysis by solving for "Sell Put."

$$\text{Sell Put} = \text{Sell Bond} + \text{Sell Call} + \text{Buy Stock}$$

where the present value of the Bond = $E(1+r)^{-t}$ and r is the default free interest rate and there are t years to maturity.

For the example where the exercise price is $11 and the maturity value of the stock is $6, selling the put resulted in a cash outlay of $5 at maturity of the put. The bond has a value of a $11 outlay (equal to the exercise price), a call with an exercise price of $11 has zero value, and the stock has a value of $6. The net value of the right hand side is a negative value of $5, thus equivalent to the outlay with a put at time t.

$$\text{Right Side of Equation} = -11 - 0 + 6 = -\$5.$$

Thus selling the put is the equivalent to issuing a bond, selling a call option on the common stock, and buying a share of stock.

Since the company repurchasing stock is buying stock, this would be equivalent to selling a put if the company also issued a bond and issued a call. But the objective is not to double the effects of the share repurchase, but rather to reduce the cost. Unfortunately, the selling of puts merely reduces the immediate net cash outlay, but leaves the cost associated with the put obligation at maturity of the put.

Hedging Share Repurchase

Assume a company wants to buy its own stock at today's price but has to wait t periods until the purchase takes place. To lock in today's price it can:

Buy $E(1+r)^{-t}$ of debt maturing at time t
Buy a call option with exercise price of E with
the call maturing at time t

<u>Example</u>

Assume E = $40, r = .06, t = 1 and at maturity the stock price is $50. The initial stock price is $40. The firm can buy the stock at a cost of $40 or alternatively the firm can buy debt and a call and sell a put at a net cost for the three transactions of $40.

Buying the stock at time 1 would cost $50 thus the firm saves $50 by buying at a $40 price at time 0. But the hedge that costs $40 pays off at time 1:

Payoff of debt	+$40
Payoff of call	+ 10
Payout for put	0
Net payoff	+$50

At time 1 the $50 saving from having bought the stock at time 0 is matched by the $50 net payoff of the hedge. At time 0 the stock would have cost $40. The hedge (debt, call, and put) must also cost $40 since the payoffs of the stock and the hedge at time 1 are the same as for the stock. Thus the one share of repurchased stock effectively costs $40 even though the cash outlay for the stock at time one is $50 (balanced by a $50 net payoff from the hedge.) The firm can buy debt, buy a call, and sell a put instead of buying the stock at time 0.

Now let the stock price at time 1 be $30. The cash saving at time 1 for the share repurchase at time 0 is $30.

The hedge also pays off $30 at time 1:

Payoff of debt	+$40
Payoff of call	+ 0
Pay-out for put	- 10
Net Payoff	$ 30

At time 1 the $30 saving for the share repurchase is matched by the $30 net payoff of the hedge. At time 0 the stock would have cost $40 thus the hedge (debt, call and put) must also cost $40 since the payoffs of the stock and the hedge are the same.

While the strategy illustrated above works perfectly it might not be possible to buy a call and sell a put both with an exercise price of E and maturity at time 1. It should be feasible to buy a default free debt security paying E at time 1. If the cost of the hedge is not equal to today's stock price there is an arbitrage opportunity involving the hedging securities and the stock.

Assume it is feasible to execute perfectly the hedge. Should the corporation want to lock in the time 0 stock price as the cost of the repurchase? Given transaction costs, the total cost will exceed the initial stock price. There is also the consideration that the stock price might be lower at time 1 than at time 0. The objective of this section is not to judge the desirability of the strategy, but rather to illustrate that it is feasible to buy a stock at today's price even though the actual stock purchase will not take place until the future. The hedge securities will be purchased today.

Some firms exercise only a portion of the hedging strategy. They do not buy debt and do not buy a call option. They do sell a put. Thus, rather than an outlay at time 0 there is a positive cash flow. Rather than locking in today's price, because of the put's payout, the strategy insures that the stock will not be purchased at a price less than E.

Conclusions

A sale of puts combined with a stock repurchase at the current market price guarantees that the company will not purchase back shares at a lower cost than (Current Market – Put Proceeds.) It might well pay more than this amount. When the stock price goes below the exercise price the amount that the company pays per share will go up from the minimum cost that was set by the sale of the puts.

Given the uncertainty that exists regarding stock market prices and the price of any individual security, management cannot be sure that the stock of its firm will always go up. The sale of the puts to reduce the cost of a share repurchase, is at best a speculative act.

The sale of a put may be part of a transaction to hedge a share repurchase. To lock in today's stock price a firm can buy debt, buy a call option and sell a put. Since this transaction, assuming the right exercise prices, maturity dates, and amount of debt, is the equivalent to buying the stock it is not clear why the firm would not merely buy the stock. If the firm only sells the put, that is merely speculation.

Chapter 12

A Ranking of Alternatives

A corporation that has generated profits has many different ways of rewarding its stockholders. Not all corporations should have the same distribution policies. Corporations should design their financial policies to accommodate the needs of different investment clienteles.

The Dividend Paying Corporations

There are many people and institutions who want a steady, possibly growing, stream of cash flows. If these investors are not taxed heavily their needs should be satisfied by cash dividends paid by corporations which have matured and where their cash needs for capital expenditures are less than the income being generated. There should be corporations which pay out a majority of their incomes as dividends to accommodate these investors (and to maximize their stock value.)

Corporations that invest in stock prefer a distribution policy that leads to a cash dividend rather than a capital gain for the stock the corporation owns. In the United States corporations owning stock and receiving a cash dividend benefit from a 70%(or higher) dividend received deduction that effectively reduces the tax on dividends to .105 for the investing corporation with a basic corporate tax rate of .35.

Thus corporations whose stock is owned completely by zero, low tax investors, or other corporations should not avoid cash dividends.

The Growing Corporations

Now let us consider growing corporations that have attracted investors who are taxed at the highest marginal tax rates. These corporations have capital needs that equal or exceed their annual cash flows from operations.

It is interesting that the most desirable distribution policy for these firms is not to distribute anything. The optimum strategy is to retain earnings. This policy saves transaction costs for both the corporation and its stockholders and saves investor taxes. Retaining earnings for projects that earn more than the investor can earn (with comparable risk) after tax is the optimum strategy. The market will tend to increase the stock price in recognition of the profitable projects being financed with the retained earnings.

But sometimes the market's estimate of value and management's expectations diverge. If the firm's stock is undervalued by the market the firm has the option of repurchasing its shares as part of a value enhancement strategy.

If management thinks that the firm's stock price is too high as a result of retention and share repurchase there are the alternatives of stock dividends and stock splits to bring down the stock price.

The Growing Corporations with Excess Cash

Consider growing corporations which have excess cash or alternatively growing corporations which feel that their investors deserve a cash distribution. What form should the cash distribution take?

A cash dividend on common stock should not be initiated (except for a modest dividend to satisfy the legal requirements of a trust list). If it has been decided that a cash distribution is desirable there are several sensible alternatives. One is a share repurchase program in lieu of a cash dividend. Secondly, to accommodate the desires of common stock investors who want a steady cash flow stream and do not object to income taxed at ordinary rates, the opportunity to exchange common stock into either preferred stock or debt is desirable.

The Corporations Currently Paying a Cash Dividend

What should corporations do that are currently paying cash dividends? These corporations should decide whether they should aim for low tax rate investors who want cash flow. If so they should maintain or increase their dividends. This strategy is appropriate if the corporation has more cash flow than it can use and it wants to aim its common stock strategy towards this specific investment group.

If the corporation has good growth investment opportunities and needs equity capital approximately equal to its cash flow from operations, then the corporation should consider a dividend reduction or elimination. This action should be accompanied by a share repurchase program (to absorb those shares held by investors who are dissatisfied with the dividend reduction) and the firm should offer an opportunity for investors wanting cash flow to exchange their common stock into preferred stock or debt.

When Dividend Reduction is Not Feasible

When the dividend reduction is not feasible, and the corporation needs equity capital, a dividend reinvestment plan is a sensible method for facilitating the raising of equity capital from the firm's common stockholders. Of course, this implies that the DRIP be implemented by the issuance of new shares (or shares held by the corporation) rather than shares purchased in the stock markets.

When the Corporation Does Not Have Good Real Investment Opportunities

Assume the corporation does not have good real investment opportunities. That is, the firm's real internal investments offer returns smaller than the comparable risk after tax returns available to the stockholders.

One possibility is for this corporation to return the equity capital to its stockholders using a share repurchase mechanism or a cash dividend.

A second possibility that has been executed brilliantly by Warren Buffet and his firm Berkshire-Hathaway is to buy the common stock and other securities of well managed firms. The percentage of ownership acquired may be small initially but may grow to a complete ownership of the common stock of the target firm.

This strategy is the equivalent to the retained earnings strategy where the firm has good internal real investments. The stock investment in Berkshire-Hathaway has the advantages for the investor of no taxes on the dividends (there are no dividends and no capital gains taxes unless the investor chooses to trigger a capital gains by selling the Berkshire-Hathaway stock).

An Exit Strategy

If the corporation promises never to pay a cash distribution to its common stock investors, the value of the common stock is zero. But the cash distribution might take a form that is different from the corporation writing a check for its stockholders.

One way the corporation might enhance the liquidity of its stockholders is for the corporation to sell itself to another corporation for cash. This exit strategy results in one unique capital gains for its common stockholders. The tax on the capital gains has been deferred until the sale of the corporations. Thus the sale of a corporation for cash is analogous to a terminal dividend with the advantage that the proceeds from the sale in excess of the investment's cost (or more exactly, the tax basis) are taxed at the capital gains rate.

Clienteles

The primary point regarding the distribution policy of a firm is that each firm should have a financial personality that is well known by the financial community. If investors know the financial policies of a firm then each investor can invest in the common stock of firms that have distribution policies that are consistent with the investor's objectives. One objective is to invest in firms whose distribution policies are reasonably tax efficient.

Consider the following matching of distribution policies and tax status.

Distribution Policy	Tax Status of Primary Investors
1. Retained Earnings	High tax investors
2. High dividend payment	a. Low on zero tax investors b. Corporate investors
3. Mix of dividend and retained earnings	a. Low or zero investors b. Corporate investors
4. Mix of share repurchase and retained earnings	a. High tax investors b. Low or zero tax investors
5. Only share repurchase	a. High tax investors b. Low or zero tax investors

Tax Status of Corporate Investors

The high dividend paying stocks and the firms with a mix of dividends and retained earnings should attract corporate investors because of the dividend received deductions. Assume the dividend received deduction is .70, then the amount of dividends subject to the .35 corporate tax rate is .30 of earnings. The effective tax rate on the dividends received by a corporation is .105:

$$.35 \ (1-.7) = .105.$$

Dividends, compared to share repurchase, are not disadvantageous to corporate investors.

Retained earnings have the advantage that the tax may be deferred and only paid in the future. Thus a combination of dividends and retained earnings is acceptable to corporate investors.

A mix of share repurchase and retained earnings offers the possibility of tax deferral but is not very attractive since any gain will be taxed at the capital gains rate for corporations.

In many situations the investor will not be able to form a well-diversified portfolio without ignoring the preferences of distribution policy in order to achieve the desired diversification. This investment strategy driven by tax strategy might have to be compromised in order to achieve a desired amount of risk diversification.

Share Buybacks as a Speculation

The stock price decreases of the year 2000 focused the attention of newspaper stock market reporters on share buybacks that resulted in "losses" for corporations. Define a loss from share buybacks to be the situation when a corporation's stock is selling at a lower price than when the shares were repurchased. Thus *The Wall Street Journal* (18 December, 2000) reported that AT & T, General Motors, Gillette, Hewlett-Packard, IBM, McDonald's, and others had losses as large as $2.5 billion in the year 2000 from buying their own stock. The practice of buying back stock when it was expensive was labeled as being "dumb."

First, there is the question of defining when a stock is selling at more than its value (thus is expensive). If one can identify overvalued stock one does not have to work for a living.

Secondly, a corporation with too much cash and a desire to return the cash to investors has two primary choices, it can pay a cash dividend or it can do a share repurchase. No one has suggested delaying a cash dividend until the stock price falls, and this logic applies equally to a share repurchase. If the firm's objective is to distribute cash to its shareholders then the relative size of market price and intrinsic value is not relevant to the repurchase decision.

Third, a corporation with too little debt and few investment opportunities might decide to finance share repurchases with debt. If the stock price then goes down, one should not conclude that the firm has made a mistake.

It is possible to imagine a corporation that needs cash and has no debt capacity but does a share repurchase expecting the stock price to increase. When the stock decreases instead of increasing and the firm must raise capital by issuing common stock, we can conclude that the firm was speculating when it did its share repurchase. The mere fact that a firm's stock price decreases after a share repurchase does not prove the firm made a mistake. Obviously, if the firm could have forecasted the stock price decline it would probably have delayed its share repurchase, but the ability of corporations to forecast stock prices, even its own, is very limited.

The *New York Times* (17 December 2000) had an article "Buybacks for the Wrong Reasons" by Gretchen Morgenson. The article concerned the share buyback of Papa John's International corporation. The buyback price was $25 and then the stock price fell to $19.69.

As a result of the buyback, financed to a large extent by debt, the firm's earnings per share had increased. The article concludes that the market was excessively optimistic regarding the firm's future as a result of the EPS increase caused by the buyback. Miss Morgenson is correct in recognizing the distinction between EPS increases that are the result of operations, especially sales increases, and increases that are the result of stock buybacks. If EPS increases as a result of sales increases, then the opportunity to also do share buybacks is increased, so there are two sources of stock value increases. If the EPS increase is the result of a share buyback and this is the only source of value per share increase, then obviously a major source of stock price increase is missing. But the increase arising from share buyback may be the only positive alternative to the firm.

Anytime a firm issues debt it is increasing risk (unless it can earn a risk free return with the debt proceeds that is larger than the cost of debt). The debt proceeds can be used to finance inventory or receivables, to buy real assets, to finance a cash dividend, or to repurchase stock. After any of these events it can be concluded that the corporation made a mistake. On the other hand, at the time of the decision there can be situations where the issuance of debt to do any of the above is a reasonable and correct decision.

A Partial LBO

The conventional LBO buys 100% of a firm's common stock. If management is part of the LBO group it will own a significant percentage of the private equity capital. The main problems are raising the private equity and accomplishing the LBO without attracting competition.

Now assume management has a different strategy. The corporation will repurchase its own shares. The stockholders who want cash receive it by selling some of their stock and having the gain on the stock sale taxed at a capital gains rate.

Assume that management currently owns or has rights (options) to 20% of the firm's 1,000,000 outstanding shares. The firm repur-chases 30% of the 1,000,000 outstanding shares. There are 700,000 shares outstanding after the share repurchase. If management does not sell any of their shares they will now own 28.57% of the shares (before the buyback they owned 20%).

$$\frac{200,000}{700,000} = .2857.$$

Obviously, if the firm continues the buyback strategy, and if management does not sell any of its shares, its percentage of ownership will increase. In a few years management will have the same percentage of ownership that it would have obtained with an immediate LBO. An important advantage of the partial LBO strategy is that management's investment is highly liquid compared to an investment in a LBO.

Conclusions

The present value of the after tax proceeds that are available to a corporation's stockholders very much depends on the form that the distributions take. When the world was somewhat simpler the common stock dividend and the dividend yield paid by the corporation were carefully watched measures since they were good indicators of stock value. Today, it is likely that the safer common stock investments will have a lower dividend yield than the higher yielding stocks. There a better understanding that the total return (dividend plus common stock price appreciation) is more important that just the dividend yield. In addition, it is necessary to consider the tax effects and the after tax returns of different investment alternatives.

If investors in a high tax bracket expect the price of a stock to increase because of improved earnings (and a higher level of future dividends), they will be willing to pay more for a stock knowing that if their expectations are realized the stock can be sold and be taxed at the relatively lower capital gains tax rate. Whereas the lower capital gains tax rate tends to increase the value of a share of stock, we have shown that another powerful factor arises from the ability of the stockholder to defer paying taxes if the corporation retains income rather than paying dividends. Tax deferral is an extremely important advantage associated with the retention of earnings by a corporation.

The present tax law allows deferral of tax payment (or complete avoidance) on capital gains, and recognized gains are taxed at a lower (0.20) rate than ordinary income. Dividend policies of firms have relevance for public policy in the areas of taxation of both corporations and individuals. As corporate managers adjust their decision making to include the tax law considerations, the makers of public policy must decide whether the results are beneficial to society.

It is not being argued that all firms should discontinue dividend payments. There is a place for a variety of payout policies, but there is a high cost to investors for firms attempting to cater to the dividend and reinvestment preferences of an average investor. The firm that com-bines dividend payments with the issuance of securities to current investors is causing some of its investors to pay unnecessary taxes, as well as incurring increased transaction costs itself in raising the funds.

A board of directors acting in the interests of the stockholders of a corporation sets the dividend policy of a firm. The ability of an investor to defer income taxes as a result of the company retaining earnings is an important consideration. In addition, the distinction between ordinary income and capital gains for purposes of income taxation by the federal government accentuates the importance of investors knowing the dividend policy of the firm whose stock they are considering purchasing or have already purchased. In turn, this means that the corporation (and its board) has a responsibility to announce its dividend policy, and attempt to be consistent in its policy, changing only when its economic situation changes significantly. In the particular situation in which a firm is expanding its investments rapidly and is financing this expansion by issuing securities to its stockholders, the payment of cash dividends is especially vulnerable to criticism.

Investment decisions, capital structure, and dividend policy must be coordinated so that the well being of the firm's stockholders is considered in the planning process. The corporate planners should realize that the individual investors are also making plans, and the corporation can assist this planning process by making its own financial plans and strategies well known.

References

Baker, H. K. and G. E. Powell, "How Corporate Managers View Dividend Policy," *Quarterly Journal of Business and Economics*, v 38 n 2 (Spring 1999), pp 17-35

Lease, R. C., *Dividend Policy: Its Impact on Firm Value*, Harvard Business School Press, Boston, 1999 (Financial Management Association Survey and Synthesis Series.

Marseguerra, G., *Corporate Financial Decisions and Market Value*, Physica-Verlag, Heidelberg, 1998

Miller, M. H. and K. Rock, "Dividend Policy Under Asymmetric Information," *The Theory of Corporate Finance*, Volume 1, Elgar, Cheltenham, U.K., 1996.

Index